GRANT MONEY
AND
HOW TO GET IT

GRANT MONEY
AND
HOW TO GET IT
A Handbook for Librarians

Richard W. Boss

R. R. Bowker Company
New York & London, 1980

Published by R. R. Bowker Company
1180 Avenue of the Americas, New York, N.Y. 10036
Copyright © 1980 by Xerox Corporation
All rights reserved
Printed and bound in the United States of America

Library of Congress Cataloging in Publication Data
Boss, Richard W
    Grant money and how to get it.
    Bibliography: p.
    Includes index.
    1. Library fund raising. I. Title.
Z683.B67   025.1'1   80-17880
ISBN 0-8352-1274-2

CONTENTS

PREFACE

This book is the result of the realization by the author and a number of professional colleagues that they knew very little about starting to seek external funds to support new programs—in other words, how to get grant money. In fact, we were overwhelmed by the complexity and scale of the effort made by those perceived to be highly successful. The author subsequently gathered information from a variety of sources, and after several years of proposal writing discovered that the process had become much easier and the success rate much higher as his understanding increased. The pressures of an administrative position do not allow much time for proposal writing. It was, therefore, necessary to assemble the information for use of others.

The author undertook a career change before the task was completed. But, to his surprise, in his new role as an information systems consultant, he continued to encounter the need for an overview of the grantsmanship process. Library clients interested in automated systems, large micrographic facilities, or video-disk technologies often lack the financial resources to implement their plans. It therefore became commonplace to provide information on obtaining external funding from foundations, government agencies, and corporations.

This book, which is a handbook of grantsmanship, is not written for experienced grant seekers. Nor does it attempt to trace the history of foundation, government, and corporate giving. It is not a catalog of sources for grants, although many funding sources interested in libraries are identified. It is, instead, an attempt to describe the process of grantsmanship, the art of identifying and getting external funds; in other words, how to get grant money.

Only a small percentage of all proposals produce checks. This book seeks to decrease the odds of failure. Some readers may decide that the tone is somewhat pessimistic because it emphasizes the difficulty of getting money and the amount of time and effort required even in a program that is consistently only 10 percent successful. But the author's view is that it is realistic to accept this high degree of failure as normal. What is not "normal" is to fail because one has not researched the prospective grantor properly or because one has not learned the many techniques practiced by the most successful grant seekers. A program may remain only 10 percent successful, but why not try to insure that you will be included in that admittedly small number? Someone is; why not you?

Success is often measured in percentages. In most undertakings, a 10 to 20 percent success rate is not very good, but in grantsmanship it can be very good indeed, generating hundreds of thousands of dollars per year. This means writing many proposals, but not a great many because most of the prospective grantors will be eliminated during the preliminary research stage. Also, much of the effort is not wasted. Proposal ideas can be rewritten and resubmitted. Statements of qualifications and methodology can often be used again and again with only minor modifications. The effort can be most worthwhile for the librarians determined to become skilled grant seekers.

The author gratefully acknowledges The Foundation Center for reference sources made available in preparing this work and Lesley M. Stern for providing material for Appendix 3.

ACRONYMS USED
IN THIS BOOK

CLR	Council on Library Resources
CFDA	*Catalog of Federal Domestic Assistance*
DIST	Division of Information Science and Technology
ESEA	Elementary and Secondary Education Act
FAPRS	Federal Assistance Programs Retrieval System
GSA	General Services Administration
HEA	Higher Education Act
HEW	Department of Health, Education, and Welfare
IRS	Internal Revenue Service
LSCA	Library Services and Construction Act
NASA	National Aeronautics and Space Administration
NDEA	National Defense Education Act
NEA	National Endowment for the Arts
NEH	National Endowment for the Humanities
NHPRC	National Historical Publications and Records Commission
NIE	National Institute of Education
NIH	National Institutes of Health
NSF	National Science Foundation
OMB	Office of Management and Budget
RFP	Requests for Proposals

1
Introduction: What Is Grantsmanship?

Bᴵᴸᴸᴵᴼᴺˢ ᴼꜰ ᴅᴼᴸᴸᴬᴿˢ—well over $33 billion annually—are available in the form of grants and contracts from private foundations, government agencies, and corporations. Yet only a few hundred of the nation's more than 100,000 libraries augment internal budgetary appropriations with externally solicited funds. There is keen competition for this money. Program officers estimate that 75 to 80 percent of all applications are rejected. Nevertheless, some libraries are successful again and again.

It is the purpose of this book to assist librarians and library staff in competing for grant funds, especially at a time when it is extremely difficult to obtain increases in budgets that exceed the rate of inflation. *Grantsmanship* has been defined as the knack of knowing where the money is and how to get it, which implies that grants are awarded less on merit than on the ability of the applicant to write good proposals. The view here is that both merit and proposal writing skill are essential to success, because there are so many competing applications.

There are well-documented reasons for the failure of many grant proposals. This book will identify the most common causes of failure and offer advice that should increase a library's success rate. Few librarians will be successful more than half the time, but a 10 percent rate is now bringing some libraries more than $1 million each per year. Careful development of institutional objectives, systematic research into potential funding sources, and skillful proposal writing can improve a library's chances for funding. One major public library more than tripled its income from grants in less than four years by formalizing the grantsmanship process.

Public tax support as the principle source of funding American libraries is a twentieth-century phenomenon. Virtually all the great libraries established in the seventeenth, eighteenth, and nineteenth centuries were developed with private gifts of money, books, and buildings. A number of academic libraries continue to depend on gifts for significant portions of their acquisitions budgets and physical facilities, but virtually all libraries open to the general public receive little more than tax support.

It is not difficult to see why tax support would displace other kinds of support. Tax support is more dependable from year to year, at least up to the level of previous years, and many potential donors do not contribute because they assume that the needs are already being met if the library appears to be well administrated.

In those academic institutions where fund raising is a significant activity, much of the work is done by professionally staffed development offices. The library staff prepare budget requests much like their counterparts in tax-supported institutions. Much of the budget of the library comes from income earned from endowment that has been invested for many years. Library staffs in privately supported institutions generally have not developed sophisticated fund-raising skills.

Librarians skilled in grantsmanship may be few in number, but they are found in all sizes and types of libraries. Some have support from an institutional development office, but the true effectiveness of each one is due to the time spent learning the fundamentals—by reading, talking, and trying. Some foundation officers claim that more than 80 percent of the grant applications they receive reflect serious misunderstandings about the funding policies and procedures of the organization. Lack of information, rather than lack of sophisticated skills, reduces most applicants' chances.

The underlying philosophy is that fund raising should be undertaken on a long-term, ongoing basis. The time and cost of developing a successful grantsmanship program can be justified only by making regular applications for funds. And paradoxical as it may seem, institutions that solicit funds each year are the ones with the highest success rates in fund raising. Institutions that have a record of external support are the most likely to receive favorable consideration concerning grants or contracts from foundations, government agencies, and corporations.

A *grant* may be an award to do research, a stipend for training or travel, or the provision of funds for construction or purchase of equipment. One of the characteristics of a grant is that it supports the grantee to do something that is important to it. The grant cannot be just a procurement of services by the grantor.

For agreements that call for the performance of a specified service or preparation of a product (a report or a piece of equipment), the term *contract* is more appropriate.

Research may be carried out under a grant or a contract. One federal agency distinguishes on the basis of whether research is supported (a grant) or procured (a contract). Foundations and corporations usually award grants. Government agencies award many research contracts as well as grants. Federal agencies always use contracts when dealing with for-profit organizations, but they give grants to nonprofit organizations to support research ideas that have been defined by the grantee.

Chapter 2 describes principal sources of funds, and following chapters detail recommended steps for systematic fund raising from foundations, government agencies, and corporations. The appendixes contain directories for Foundation Center regional collections, state and federal sources and agencies, Department of Education regional centers,* and all-important foundation profiles. Also included are a glossary, a list of acronyms, and a bibliography

*These centers were originally organized under the Department of Health, Education, and Welfare (HEW). In June 1980, HEW was reorganized into the Department of Education and the Department of Human Services. Although further reorganization of the regional centers may occur, it is expected that their addresses will remain the same.

2

Sources of Funds

THE THREE MAIN sources of funds are private foundations, government (mainly federal) agencies, and corporations. Private foundations distribute more than $2.1 billion* per year and government agencies more than $30 billion. For corporate giving, $2 billion is probably a realistic figure.

A *foundation* is a nonprofit, nongovernmental organization that has as its primary purpose the making of grants. The foundation's funds are normally administered by trustees or directors subject to whatever guidelines or purposes have been prescribed by the person or persons who established the foundation.

A *government agency* may be any unit of federal, state, county, or municipal government. The emphasis here, however, is on the 100 federal agencies that distribute almost all of the grant and contract funds.

A *corporation* is any business organized for profit, but the emphasis here is on large corporations, which have the greatest potential for solicitation by libraries.

Foundations

It is important to differentiate between public and private foundations.

The public foundation usually engages in current fund raising to support its grant giving. Sources of funds are generally numerous. The American Cancer Society and the United Way are examples of public

*Giving USA, 1978 (New York: American Association of Fund-Raising Counsel, Inc., 1979).

4

foundations active throughout the country, but there are also many small local groups. Public foundations do not have to pay excise taxes (the duties imposed on goods and services produced within the country). Private foundations secure most of their funds from a limited number of sources. In fact, most of them realize current income from earnings on the investment of their initial endowment. Private foundations pay excise taxes on their investment incomes and are required to dispose of at least 6 percent of the market value of their assets each year. Private foundations are concentrated on here because they are the principal sources of grants to libraries.

TYPES OF PRIVATE FOUNDATIONS

There are several types of private foundations: general purpose, special purpose, community, corporate, and family.

General-purpose foundations seek to support a broad range of activities and are normally the wealthiest. Some 400 of these foundations have over 60 percent of all private foundation assets and give out nearly half of all the foundation grants each year. The top 2,800 foundations make grants totaling over $1.5 billion in a single year, including virtually all grants over $100,000.* Examples of general-purpose foundations are Carnegie, Ford, and Mellon.

Special-purpose foundations are established to give money for a specific type of activity or in a limited locality. There are thousands of them, but most have only small amounts of money. Examples of special-purpose foundations are the Robert Wood Johnson Foundation (health care) and the Exxon Education Foundation (higher education).

Community foundations provide a means for specific areas to draw on local capital to meet local needs. A community foundation is local in scope and normally has a broad base of local donors. There are approximately 250 community foundations in the United States. A single staff coordinate the giving of many donors to a wide variety of activities. Although most are small, the Cleveland Foundation and the Chicago and New York Community Trusts have grown to more than $100 million each in assets. The assets of all community foundations now exceed $1.5 billion and are growing rapidly. Each year these foundations distribute more than $87 million.

There are at least 1,500 corporate foundations in the United States. Each corporate foundation is legally independent of its sponsor, but there are often many corporate officers on the foundation board. Although corporate foundations have less than 7 percent of all foundation assets, they are particularly significant in the field of higher education, where

*Foundation Directory (New York: Foundation Center, 1979, seventh ed.).

Table 1   Foundations by Asset Size*

Asset Size	No.
$100 million or more	32
$10 million to $100 million	382
$1 million to $10 million	2,563
Under $1 million	23,455

*Bowker Annual, 1977 (New York: R. R. Bowker Co., 1977), p. 217.

they focus their support. They are also increasing their assets faster than the other foundation types. The Xerox Foundation is an example of a large corporate foundation, as are the Ford Motor Company Fund, and Atlantic Richfield, Alcoa, and United States Steel foundations. One of the provisions of the 1969 Tax Reform Act made it illegal for a foundation to make gifts that are primarily beneficial to the corporation. Therefore, despite the presence of company officers on the board, commonly the ties with the original funding source are quite loose.

Family foundations represent over 80 percent of the total number in the nation. Many are small. Collectively, family foundations (the Baker [George F.] Trust is an example) have only 15 percent of the total assets of private foundations. Family foundations usually have narrow interests, in terms of both the type of activities supported and the geographic area covered. Seventy percent of the family foundations focus their giving locally as against 41 percent of the company foundations, so that company foundations are usually the first ones that should be investigated when a person does not reside in a state with a significant concentration of foundations.

NUMBER OF PRIVATE FOUNDATIONS

Approximately 27,000 nonprofit organizations were classified as private foundations by the Internal Revenue Service (IRS) in 1974. The number decreased to 26,000 in 1979.* The majority of these have limited resources and limited topical or geographic interests. In fact, the Foundation Center estimated that 7,000 make no appreciable grants and are of little interest to grant seekers.† The preponderance of small private foundations is illustrated in Table 1.

Approximately 1,000 private foundations hold 90 percent of all foundation assets. Although the number of grants made in a year exceeds 100,000, less than 15,000 of them total more than $5,000. Almost all of these are given out by the 1,000 largest private foundations. In fact,

*Wall Street Journal, August 10, 1979, p. 1.

†Foundation Center, National Data Bank (New York: Foundation Center, 1979), p. 5.

giving is even more high concentrated. Less than 200 of the largest foundations holding 65 percent of the assets give 14 percent (30,434) of the grants (216,385) but, in aggregate, 51 percent of the dollars. The average size of grants from this group is relatively large: $53,873 for foundations with assets of $100 million or more and $19,680 for foundations between $25 and $100 million. Conversely, a large number of small foundations (2,939) hold a third of the assets and give almost half of the grant dollars, but they divide the money into smaller grants (185,951), averaging from $3,000 to $11,000 each.*

Foundations are concentrated in the more industrial Middle Atlantic and East North Central regions of the country. New York State alone has 667, Pennsylvania 212, Ohio 224, and Illinois 207. Only California with 249, Texas with 175, and Massachusetts with 135 have significant numbers of foundations outside these two regions.

SUPPORT TO LIBRARIES

It is not unusual each year for the vast majority of private foundation grants to libraries to come from foundations in such states as California, Connecticut, Massachusetts, Michigan, New York, Pennsylvania, and Texas, plus the District of Columbia. The competition for funds is also keenest in these areas. It may be easier to get one of 10 grants awarded to libraries in Florida than one of 42 awarded to libraries in Michigan. (For how libraries fare in grant money, see Table 2.)

Twenty private foundations made grants of $400,000 or more to libraries in 1976. The total of 481 grants in 1975–1976 was only 2.1 percent of the total number of private foundation grants made during the period. The average amount per library grant was $79,977.† The large majority of grants to libraries were under $50,000, and very few exceeded $1 million. In 1979 the number of grants made to libraries by major private foundations was 403, for a total of $36.5 million.‡

There are a number of private foundations with a stated interest in libraries. Appendix 2 contains a brief description of each of the private foundations, as well as those with a history of making grants to libraries. The data in Appendix 2 was drawn from tax returns, published annual reports, and Foundation Center materials. Many of the returns for the more recent years have not yet been distributed by the IRS and some foundations have not yet supplied recent data to The Foundation

---

*Data from Thomas R. Buckman, "The Status of Foundations—1979," *Foundation News,* November/December 1979, p. 29.

†Ibid.

‡*Bowker Annual, 1980* (New York: R. R. Bowker Co., 1980), p. 278.

Table 2 Foundation Funding of Libraries by State*

State	Dollars Given	No. Given	Dollars Recd.	No. Recd.
Alabama	—	—	—	—
Alaska	—	—	—	—
Arizona	—	—	$ 55,000	2
Arkansas	—	—	—	—
California	$ 3,666,468	33	6,394,635	46
Colorado	10,000	2	49,026	3
Connecticut	1,159,164	7	2,547,980	10
Delaware	—	—	—	—
District of Columbia	690,906	19	2,748,406	23
Florida	442,682	10	499,682	10
Georgia	350,000	2	967,778	12
Hawaii	—	—	—	—
Idaho	—	—	30,000	1
Illinois	468,560	12	998,571	17
Indiana	911,221	6	554,000	3
Iowa	—	—	34,000	2
Kansas	—	—	95,434	3
Kentucky	—	—	53,800	3
Louisiana	—	—	—	—
Maine	—	—	83,000	1
Maryland	—	—	25,000	1
Massachusetts	75,000	1	2,317,445	20
Michigan	7,217,846	42	2,872,798	21
Minnesota	248,000	8	150,00	5
Mississippi	—	—	—	—
Missouri	5,000	1	15,000	1
Montana	—	—	—	—
Nebraska	—	—	50,882	1
Nevada	430,000	2	390,000	1
New Hampshire	—	—	10,000	1
New Jersey	126,000	7	187,000	7
New Mexico	—	—	15,000	1
New York	13,562,165	158	7,731,207	79
North Carolina	—	—	533,090	10
North Dakota	—	—	—	—
Ohio	85,000	4	200,000	8
Oklahoma	1,061,400	3	500,000	1
Oregon	—	—	—	—
Pennsylvania	3,440,073	48	2,082,204	44
Rhode Island	5,000	1	30,000	3
South Carolina	—	—	—	—
South Dakota	—	—	30,000	2
Tennessee	—	—	15,000	2
Texas	2,434,319	32	2,874,319	30
Utah	—	—	49,731	2
Vermont	—	—	100,000	1
Virginia	—	—	373,500	8
Washington	30,000	2	350,316	4
West Virginia	—	—	10,000	2
Wisconsin	82,500	3	7,500	1
Wyoming	—	—	—	—
Total	$36,501,304	403	$36,031,304	392

*Bowker Annual, 1980 (New York: R. R. Bowker Co., 1980), p. 280.

Center; therefore, information for some of the listings in the appendix is dated.

Contrary to public opinion, foundation grants to libraries do not go almost exclusively to private academic institutions. The pattern that prevailed in 1979 is shown in Table 3.

Table 3   Library Grants by Type of Library*

Type of Library	Amt.	Percent	No. of Grants
Academic	$20,532,012	56	189
Special	8,385,191	23	79
Library networks and associations	3,410,387	9	13
Public	2,424,764	7	74
Other (nonprofit organizations, etc.)	847,967	2	16
Government agencies	440,208	1	9
School	422,327	1	20
Library of Congress	38,448	less than 1	3
Total	$36,501,304	100	403

Bowker Annual, 1980 (New York: R. R. Bowker Co., 1980), p. 278.

The pattern of grant awards is more one of large contributions flowing to distinguished libraries, academic, public, and special, that have maintained active grantsmanship programs over a number of years (see Table 4).

The acquisition of materials was once the principal purpose of foundation aid. Now, all types of support are given, as indicated in Table 5.

Government Agencies

The agencies of the U.S. government distribute more than $30 billion in grant and contract funds each year. More than 1,000 agencies are involved, making the identification of funding sources as complicated as seeking private foundation support. Less than 100 agencies award more than 90 percent of the nonmilitary grants and contracts.

Government agencies require much more detailed applications than do private foundations. The review process is also more complex and time consuming.

The first-known federal grant was probably the one made to Samuel F. B. Morse, Jr., in the mid-1800s to test the feasibility for public use of the electromagnetic telephone system, but the present level of federal grant making dates back to the early 1960s. In 1969 an estimated two-thirds of the more than 420 grant programs in existence at that time had been authorized since 1963.*

*U.S. Congress, House Committee on Government Operations, Subcommittee on Intergovernmental Relations, *Grant Consolidation and Intergovernmental Relations,* June 1969.

Table 4   Leading Library Recipients of Foundation Grants*

Institution	Grant Amt.	No. of Grants
New York Public Library		
Astor (Vincent) Foundation	$ 10,000	1
Booth Ferris Foundation	100,000	1
Calder (Louis) Foundation	25,000	1
Carnegie Corporation of New York	15,000	1
Clark (Edna McConnell) Foundation	30,000	1
Commonwealth Fund	400,000	1
Corning Glass Works Foundation	26,500	1
Culpeper (Charles E.) Foundation	40,880	1
Davis (Arthur Vining) Foundation	50,000	1
Dodge (Cleveland H.) Foundation	5,000	1
Fairchild (Sherman) Foundation	50,000	1
General Motors Foundation	5,000	1
Irving One Wall Street Foundation	14,000	2
Manufacturers Hanover Foundation	43,500	2
Merck Company Foundation	5,000	1
Mobil Foundation	57,500	1
New York Times Company Foundation	22,866	1
Rubinstein (Helena) Foundation	15,000	1
S & H Foundation	20,000	1
Scherman Foundation	75,000	1
Shell Companies Foundation	5,000	1
Shubert Foundation	10,000	1
United States Steel Foundation	5,000	1
Weatherhead Foundation	50,000	1
Subtotal	$1,080,246	26
Pierpont Morgan Library		
Cary (Mary Flagler) Charitable Trust	$ 50,000	1
Heineman Foundation for Research, Educational,		
Charitable, and Scientific Purposes	3,207,688	2
Kresge Foundation	150,000	1
Kress (Samuel H.) Foundation	50,000	1
Teagle Foundation	10,000	1
United States Steel Foundation	25,000	1
Subtotal	$3,492,688	7
University of Michigan		
Aeroquip Foundation	$ 5,000	1
Benedum (Claude Worthington) Foundation	250,000	1
Kellogg (W.K.) Foundation	500,000	1
Kresge Foundation	1,500,000	2
McGregor Fund	65,000	3
Mellon (Andrew W.) Foundation	83,000	1
Pew (J. Howard) Freedom Trust	100,000	1
Subtotal	$2,503,000	10

Bowker Annual, 1980 (New York: R. R. Bowker Co., 1980), pp. 281–282.

Table 4 (cont.)

Institution	Grant Amt.	No. of Grants
Research Libraries Group		
Carnegie Corporation of New York	$ 500,000	1
Hewlett (William and Flora) Foundation	300,000	1
Mellon (Andrew W.) Foundation	1,000,000	1
Sloan (Alfred P.) Foundation	500,000	1
Subtotal	$2,300,000	4
Stanford University		
Ahmanson Foundation	$ 200,000	1
Amoco Foundation	10,000	1
Calder (Louis) Foundation	50,000	1
Kresge Foundation	500,000	1
Merrill (Charles E.) Trust	100,000	2
Pew (J. Howard) Freedom Trust	500,000	1
Scaife (Sarah) Foundation	150,000	1
Subtotal	$1,510,000	8
Trinity University		
Brown Foundation	$ 666,666	1
Clark Foundation, The	5,000	1
Houston Endowment	500,000	1
Mabee (J. E. and L. E.) Foundation	500,000	1
Subtotal	$1,671,666	4
Yale University		
Booth Ferris Foundation	$ 50,000	1
Cary (Mary Flagler) Charitable Trust	63,000	2
Mudd (Seeley G.) Fund	1,500,000	1
Subtotal	$1,613,000	4

Table 5   Library Grants by Grant Purpose*

Purpose	Amt.	Percent	No. of Grants
Buildings and equipment	$ 9,529,629	26	51
General support	8,123,886	22	131
Acquisitions and materials	6,133,502	17	79
Renovation and expansion	6,587,376	18	57
Special projects	2,626,646	7	46
Computer-related projects	2,299,563	6	12
Endowment	415,000	1	4
Publications and research	412,635	1	12
Evaluations and studies	318,419	less than 1	6
Other	33,148	less than 1	2
Fellowships and scholarships	16,500	less than 1	2
Conferences	5,000	less than 1	1
Total	$36,501,304	100	403

Bowker Annual, 1980 (New York: R. R. Bowker Co., 1980), p. 279.

One of the major factors that prompted the growth of the federal role was the launching of Sputnik by the Soviet Union in 1957. The National Aeronautics and Space Administration (NASA) was formed the following year, and billions in grants for scientific research were distributed over the next decade.

The National Defense Education Act (NDEA) of 1958 provided funds for improving teaching in languages, mathematics, and sciences. The programs included loans for college students, funds for research in education, support of institutes and training centers, and a variety of other activities.

The Elementary and Secondary Education acts (ESEA) and the Higher Education Act (HEA), both passed in 1965, broadened the base of federal support and became major sources of funds for libraries. The National Science Foundation (NSF) has also been a major source of funds, especially for research in library and information science.

Revenue sharing, which dates back to 1972, has decentralized much of the distribution of federal funds. More than half of all federal nonmilitary grants have been distributed by the Department of Health, Education, and Welfare (HEW), reorganized as of June 1980 into the Department of Education and the Department of Human Services. See Table 6 for distribution of library and related programs.

Corporations

Less than 6 percent of corporations make grants of more than $500 per year, and half of the $2 billion distributed annually comes from fewer than 1,000 companies, indicating that corporate giving is not well established. Although corporations can legally donate up to 5 percent of their pretax profits, their donations generally fall far short of that figure.

Some corporate philanthropy is dispersed through the company foundations, but the 1969 Tax Reform Act has made that less attractive than direct company grants. Direct solicitation of corporations is not yet as common as solicitation of private foundations and government agencies.

Corporations have the least formal application procedures. Personal contact is very important, more so than it is in raising funds from private foundations and government agencies. Many corporate contributions are made in kind (meaning the applicant shares in the cost by committing facilities, equipment, or personnel) or as gifts of facilities, equipment, or supplies.

There is no single source of information about corporate giving, but some generalizations can be made.

1. Traditionally, corporations make their giving plans in the fall of the year.

Table 6 Funds for Library and Related Programs*

Programs	FY 1980 Appropriation	FY 1981 Authorization	Carter FY 1981 Budget
Library Programs			
ESEA Title IV-B: School Libraries	$171,000,000[a]	Necessary Sums	$171,000,000[a]
GPO Superintendent of Documents	23,000,000	44 USC 301	26,200,000
HEA Title VI-A:Undergraduate Equipment	(0)	70,000,000	(0)
Higher Education Act: Title II	11,987,500	140,000,000	12,988,000
Title II-A: College Library Resources	4,988,000	84,000,000	4,988,000
Title II-B: Training	667,000	23,976,000	500,000
Title II-B: Demonstrations	333,000	12,024,000	500,000
Title II-C: Research Libraries	6,000,000	20,000,000	7,000,000
Library of Congress	177,491,000	2 USC 131-170	196,526,000
Library Services and Construction Act	67,500,000	170,000,000	74,500,000
Title I: Library Services	62,500,000	150,000,000	62,500,000
Title II: Public Library Construction	(0)	Necessary Sums	(0)
Title III: Interlibrary Cooperation	5,000,000	20,000,000	12,000,000
Medical Library Assistance Act	9,925,000	18,500,000	9,831,000
National Commission Library Information Science	668,000	750,000	699,000
National Library of Medicine	34,732,000	40 USC 275	34,899,000
USDA SEA Technical Information Systems[b]	7,835,000	7 USC 2204	8,789,000
Library-Related Programs			
Adult Education Act	100,000,000[a]	270,000,000	120,000,000[a]
Community Schools	3,138,000	55,000,000	3,138,000
Consumers Education	3,617,000	5,000,000	3,617,000
Corporation for Public Broadcasting	172,000,000[c]	Formula Based	182,000,000[c]
Education for Handicapped Children (state grants)	874,500,000[a]	Formula Based	922,000,000[a]
Education Information Centers	3,000,000	40,000,000	(0)
Education TV Programming	6,000,000	Necessary Sums	6,000,000
ESEA Title I: Educationally Disadvantaged Children	3,115,593,000[a]	Formula Based	3,369,772[a]

Table 6 (cont.)

Programs	FY 1980 Appropriation	FY 1981 Authorization	Carter FY 1981 Budget
ESEA Title II: Basic Skills Improvement	35,000,000	30,000,000	40,000,000
ESEA Title IV-C: Educational Innovation and Support	146,400,000[a]	Necessary Sums	146,400,000[a]
ESEA Title VII: Bilingual Education	166,963,000	999,000,000	192,000,000
ESEA Title IX: Ethnic Heritage Studies	3,000,000	15,000,000	3,000,000
Gifted and Talented Children	6,280,000	35,000,000	6,280,000
HEA Title I-A: Community Service	10,000,000	40,000,000	(0)
HEA Title I-B: Lifelong Learning	(0)	40,000,000	(0)
HEA Title III: Developing Institutions	110,000,000	120,000,000	120,000,000
HEA Title VII: Construction and Renovation	54,000,000	580,000,000	26,000,000
HEA Title IX: A&B Graduate/Professional Education Opportunities	8,850,000	Necessary Sums	13,000,000
Indian Educational Act	75,900,000	Necessary Sums	100,950,000
Metric Education	1,840,000	20,000,000	1,840,000
National Center for Educational Statistics	9,947,000	30,000,000	11,793,000
National Endowment for the Arts	154,400,000	Needs new auth.	167,960,000
National Endowment for the Humanities	150,100,000	Needs new auth.	164,325,000
National Historical Publications and Records Committee	4,000,000	4,000,000	4,000,000
National Institute of Education	77,100,000	125,000,000	88,100,000
NDEA Title VI: Foreign Language Development	17,000,000	75,000,000	23,000,000
Postsecondary Education Improvement Fund	13,500,000	75,000,000	17,000,000
Public Telecommunications Facilities	23,705,000	40,000,000	23,705,000
Teacher Centers	13,000,000	100,000,000	14,300,000
Telecommunications Demonstrations	1,000,000	1,000,000	1,000,000
Women's Education Equity	10,000,000	80,000,000	20,000,000

*ALA Washington Office, January 1980.

[a]Advance funded program.

[b]Formerly National Agricultural Library.

[c]CPB funded two years in advance.

2. Corporations give primarily to education, health, and social welfare projects.
3. Corporations prefer to make contributions in communities in which they have plants or offices.
4. The amount of giving is often based on the number of employees the company has in the community.
5. Approximately half of all corporate contributions are made to public foundations such as the United Fund.
6. Many companies emphasize contributions to organizations in areas related to their field(s) of operation. A pharmaceutical company may focus its grants in pharmaceutical research and other medical science areas, while a high technology company might make grants to schools of engineering, computer science departments, or special library collections in the applied sciences.
7. Corporations usually reduce their level of contribution when profits are down; therefore, past patterns of giving are not always a reliable guide to future activity.
8. Corporations appear to be extremely conservative in their giving, only rarely supporting "new" projects. More than most funding sources, they fund local projects that apply techniques already successfully used elsewhere.

Basic Questions and Answers

Q. What are the main sources of grant funds?

A. Private foundations, government agencies, and corporations.

Q. What are the types and number of private foundations?

A. General purpose, special purpose, community, corporate, and family. The IRS classified approximately 26,000 nonprofit organizations as private foundations in 1979.

Q. What is the extent of private foundation support to libraries?

A. Major private foundations made 403 grants to libraries in 1979 for a total of $36.5 million.

Q. What are the basic characteristics of corporate giving?

A. Money goes primarily to education, health, and social welfare projects; there is a preference to make contributions in communities where corporate offices or plants are based.

3
Assessing Fund-Raising Chances

A<small>NY</small> FUND-RAISING effort must start with a review of what the library wishes to accomplish. Successful grantsmanship depends on finding a foundation or agency that shares the goals of the library. Unless the particular library's goals and subordinate objectives are clearly defined, the granting body may well determine the library's direction even when the two institutions do not share the same interests. This danger is particularly great in the case of federal grants, because such programs are often more sharply delineated and deviation from the conditions of the original award are more difficult than in the case of foundation grants. There may be a matching or cost-sharing requirement that may divert resources from other library programs.

A clear understanding of the goals of the library and of the granting agency can also be a major factor in obtaining funds. Many library administrators "sell" their needs to the funding source rather than demonstrating in what ways the goals of the library and of the funding source are similar. Many librarians consider all fund solicitations as selling or begging; in fact, such solicitations should be regarded as "marketing" rather than selling. A major portion of the effort is not in the presentation but in the research into a matching of library and funding agency goals.

Goals and Objectives

In the broadest sense, the terms *goals* and *objectives* mean the same thing: where does the organization wish to go and how does it wish to get there? However, "goals" as used here describe the ongoing program

16

commitments of a library and "objectives" describe the specific, observable, measurable statements of what is to be done to achieve the goals. For example, one university library adopted the following goal: Acquire and provide service for all forms of recorded information, including nonprint materials, in selected fields pertinent to the programs of the university.* This goal clearly commits the library to an active program of acquiring audio, video, and microform materials, but there is also a recognition of the need to set limits by having the library collection reflect the interests of the parent institution. It reflects the hopes and desires of those who developed the statement, but it is specific enough to permit the identification of objectives. Typical objectives might include specific provision for a percentage of the budget to be committed to nonprint acquisitions or for specific numbers of titles to be acquired within a year or other designated time period. A statement of objectives must always be measurable, so that the library or a funding source can determine what progress is being made. Not all objectives need to be measured in dollars or numbers of titles, however. Another objective consistent with the goal in this example might be the appointment of a nonprint librarian or the scheduling of a series of appointments with faculty members to discuss the potential of nonprint materials as a resource for teaching and research.

Basically, a meaningfully stated goal or objective is one that succeeds in communicating the writer's intent to the reader. It conveys to the reader a picture identical to that which the writer had in mind. A good statement is one that excludes the greatest number of possible alternatives to the goal.

Not only must one have a statement of the library's goals and objectives, but one must also identify the goals and objectives of the funding source. These "statements" rarely are separate documents so labeled. The library's statement may be drawn from a recent budget request or annual report and refined for the purpose. The statement of the funding source may be determined by reading the description of the foundation or agency in a directory, studying its annual report, examining its pattern of past awards, or talking with a company program officer.

The goals and objectives of the library should then be restated in a grant application in such a manner that the funding source will recognize the similarity to its own goals and objectives. For example, if the library has a commitment to nonprint materials and the funding agency's principal concern is the improvement of art education, stress might be placed on the acquisition of slides and films in the interpretation of the goal. All the relevant objectives would be cited, including those for cataloging,

*Bulletin from the University of Tennessee Library, March 15, 1973.

reference service, and library instruction. Each objective would be recast in the light of the funding source's special interest.

The funding source will almost always be concerned with the effect of the grant beyond the recipient institution. A library statement should, therefore, also show how its objectives are linked to those of other libraries, so that by funding this one library, the foundation or agency can help many others.

A funding agency may have a specified geographic preference, or this preference may be suggested by its past pattern of funding. A library in Seattle, for instance, is in Washington State, but it is also in the Northwest, the American West, the Washington–British Columbia region, and on the Pacific Coast. The grant application should emphasize the perspective with which the funding source will most naturally identify.

When seeking a funding source, it is well to keep these points in mind:

1. A library should review its goals and objectives and draw from them the ones that underlie the specific grant proposal being developed.
2. These goals and objectives should be compared with those of the funding source and restated to emphasize that the library's proposal will achieve the source's goals and objectives.

In summary, goals are usually abstract in content, broad in scope, and not readily measurable; they describe overall intent. Objectives are specific, concrete, measurable, and realizable in the not-too-distant future; they describe the specific accomplishments to be achieved. They must not be ambiguous.

Documentation

Chances are that library administrators will not have much difficulty finding really important needs to address. The key to translating a need into funding is not in identifying the need, but in proving that the need is pressing, yet capable of solution. A librarian should ascertain whether there is adequate documentation to demonstrate that a problem exists and whether that documentation can be dramatized. Almost every library has many deteriorating volumes, but two libraries have won large foundations grants for binding and preservation because they made their cases particularly well.

The staff of the first library undertook a random sample inventory of its collections and determined just how many volumes were in need of which kind of attention. It demonstrated that its parent institution (a university) could not alone undo the ravages of time and pollution, but was able and willing to fund internally an ongoing program of binding and preservation if the funding source would assist the library in establishing the proper facilities, training the staff, and preserving that which was in need of immediate attention.

The staff of the second institution, a public library, produced a report on the state of its collections in a compelling format: photographs of deteriorating materials reproduced on poor quality newsprint that looked and felt fragile. Great emphasis was placed on the impact of the loss of specific titles on the users of the library.

Both library staffs emphasized that the needs as defined in their proposals could be met, but that the great need of all libraries could not be met by the funding sources. Instead, they proposed to publicize their programs to awaken the interest of libraries and other funding sources. The libraries recognized that foundations and government agencies like to give grants for projects that are capable of implementation with a limited, specified amount of money. They normally wish to avoid situations that may bring the library back for continuing funding. They also like to realize long-term benefits from short-term investments.

Here again, specific objectives are useful, because they provide "closure" at the end of a grant period. The observable, measurable elements built into a good objective will help both library and funding source to determine when the target has been reached.

Funding officials like to have something to show for their grant after the funds have stopped flowing. Offering to provide a final report is routine, but offering to host an institute or to submit an article to a professional journal to share the results is even more attractive because it increases the visibility of the funding source.

It is also highly desirable to demonstrate outside support for the project or program for which funding is sought. A public library should demonstrate community input into the project design. Testimony from those who will benefit is particularly signficant when the names of the individuals or their groups are known to the funding source. One public library application for a program to educate the public about the value of the 1980 census apparently was successful because leaders of black and Hispanic groups in the community wrote strong letters of support.

It is important that funding sources be confident in the ability of the library to accomplish what it proposes to do. One reason why a small number of libraries have been funded repeatedly is that they have demonstrated their capabilities time and again. The staff of a library without an established track record must therefore assess its human resources and satisfy itself that it can do the job, and then set forth its qualifications in a persuasive way to those who do not know it.

Statistics about past successes, quotations from prominent persons, favorable mentions in the professional literature, a description of unique facilities or equipment, and the past professional experience of key library personnel will all help to establish credibility.

A library's chances are also improved if a proposed project has some flexibility. If parts of the project can be omitted and still obtain worthwhile results, the funding source has more than the option of a yes or no answer. This is not a suggestion to pad a proposal, but to make it modular, so that the funding source can fit something it finds attractive into its available budget.

Only a small number of grant proposals are funded. Frequently, several libraries propose to address the same problem, but one is selected over the others because there is something unique about its approach. A number of program officers agree that it is the ability to look at a common problem in a new way, a different approach in characterizing the institution, or a unique combination of human resources that attracts them to one proposal as against others.

The list that follows will help to determine whether a library's chances of being funded justify the considerable time and expense of preparing and submitting proposals.

The problem is significant.

The problem is common.

The problem can be documented.

The problem can be solved.

There is "closure," or an end in sight.

The results will be visible.

Outside support exists.

The qualifications of the library can be established.

The scope of the project is flexible.

The library offers something unique.

Basic Questions and Answers

Q. What are goals?

A. Goals are the ongoing program commitments of a library.

Q. What are objectives?

A. Objectives are the specific, measurable statements of what is to be done to achieve the goals.

Q. Why should goals and objectives be stated clearly in a grant application?

A. So that the funding source will recognize the similarity between its own goals and objectives and those of the library.

Q. What is documentation?

A. Demonstration that a problem exists and can be remedied or altered by the grant.

Q. How can a library staff, without a past record of successful funding, convince a funding source that it can accomplish what it proposes to do?

A. First, satisfy itself that it can do the job; then set down its qualifications in a persuasive manner, trying to approach what is perhaps a common problem in a unique way.

4
Organizing
Library Resources

It takes people and money to raise money. It is not enough to write a good idea in proposal form, obtain 50 names of foundations that support libraries, and send photocopies to each of them. Such an unfocused approach resulted in the following responses for one library:

Six foundations wrote back saying their deadline was past.

Five said the format of the proposal was not acceptable.

Ten said the amount sought exceeded their maximum grant limit.

Six declined because they limited their grants geographically.

Thirteen replied that they did not fund the type of project proposed.

Ten did not answer.

Taking careful aim on a funding source is very important because, typically, a foundation or government agency concentrates resources in only a few areas. Every funding source has its own review process, which must be known and understood so that a proposal will not be rejected for technical reasons. Almost all sources get more requests than they can handle; accordingly, they need make little effort to compensate for lack of knowledge by the requesting institution.

The Grants Coordinator

A library interested in systematic external fund raising should appoint a grants coordinator. In most cases, the assignment will be on a part-time basis, but in all cases there must be time specifically set aside for such activities as:

1. Learning the techniques of grantsmanship through reading, conference and institute attendance, and day-to-day experience.
2. Identifying sources of funds.
3. Distributing notices of opportunities to appropriate persons within the library.
4. Establishing and maintaining contacts in the organizations that are the most likely sources of funds.
5. Maintaining the "boiler plate" for proposals, such as the library's statement of qualifications.
6. Preparing or assisting in the preparations of proposals.
7. Reviewing grant proposals before they are submitted and obtaining appropriate signatures.
8. Arranging for the timely transmittal of proposals to the funding agencies.
9. Undertaking followup.
10. Dealing with funding sources on questions that may arise after the award of a grant.

A part-time grants coordinator is preferable to retaining a professional fund raiser. A fund raiser takes a proposal idea prepared by the library and develops it into a formal grant proposal. The proposal will usually be well organized and attractive in appearance, but it will often lack real substance because the writer is generally not a professional librarian. This fact may come through to the funding source in preliminary review, and the library runs the real risk of not being able to respond adequately in negotiations that follow selection by the funding source. The library may also be ill prepared to perform after a grant is awarded. The money expended for such services is better invested in the training of a grants coordinator for the library. If the library cannot do so, an alternative would be a joint venture with one or more other libraries.

Some professional proposal writers also advise applicants on funding sources. Since they concentrate on the complex pattern of federal funding, many are located in and around Washington, D.C. They may assist in arranging meetings with the appropriate agency officials and may even engage in limited lobbying. These services are costly, often over $50 per hour. Again, the same money might be better invested in developing grantsmanship skills within the library, because there will be future occasions to make grant applications.

The most effective use of a grantsmanship consultant is as a reviewer, especially of proposals for federal agencies. In this case, the applicant prepares the proposal and, prior to formal submission, sends it to the consultant for review and criticism. The consultant is usually not an expert in the field of the application, but he or she reviews it for compliance with instructions, format, style, apparent competency of the staff to undertake the project, and other factors. The consultant tries to raise the kinds of questions normally asked by a funding review committee. If the answers are not contained in the proposal in the proper place, revision of the proposal will be recommended. The fee for this service may range from about $100 to $400.

Names and addresses for the largest fund-raising counseling firms can be obtained from the membership brochure of the American Association of Fund-Raising Counsel, Inc., 500 Fifth Ave., New York, N.Y. 10036.

Some universities have established offices in Washington and in the state capitols, but again these are staffed by people with only limited knowledge of libraries. They can assist, but they cannot be effective intermediaries.

The grants coordinator, however, can be effective. The coordinator should establish a collection of basic working tools and become fully familiar with their content and use. A core collection of 12 titles, listed below, is extremely important.

1. *Annual Register of Grants Support.* Chicago: Marquis Who's Who, annual.
2. *Catalog of Federal Domestic Assistance.* Washington, D.C.: Government Printing Office, annual.
3. *Commerce Business Daily.* Washington D.C.: Government Printing Office, daily.
4. Conrad, Daniel L., *How to Get Federal Grants.* San Francisco: Public Management Institute, 1979.
5. Dun and Bradstreet's *Million Dollar Directory.* New York: Dun and Bradstreet, annual.
6. *Fortune Double 500 Directory.* Trenton, N.J.: Fortune, annual.
7. *Foundation Directory.* New York: Foundation Center, annual.
8. *Foundation Grants Index.* New York: Foundation Center, annual.
9. *Foundation News.* Washington, D.C.: Council on Foundations, bimonthly.
10. *Giving U.S.A.* New York: American Association of Fund-Raising Council, annual.
11. *Grantsmanship Center News.* Los Angeles: Grantsmanship Center, bimonthly.
12. White, Virginia, *Grants: How to Find Out About Them and What to Do Next.* New York: Plenum Press, 1975.

The twelfth listed title, *Grants: How to Find Out About Them and What to Do Next,* is the best available general book on grantsmanship. It is the one frequently mentioned by personnel of the Foundation Center, an independent, nonprofit organization that gathers data on grants and grant funders. The staff emphasize, however, that the center endorses only its own publications. (See Chapter 5 for details on the Foundation Center, its services, and publications.) Both foundation and government agency information are given in White's book. It should be read as an introduction to the process for the grants coordinator and for others who expect to be involved in the development of proposals on a regular basis.

Grantsmanship Seminars

The grants coordinator should not only become familiar with the tools already mentioned, but should also seek to enroll in a grantsmanship institute as soon as possible after his or her appointment. The nonprofit Grantsmanship Center conducts week-long grantsmanship seminars in major cities throughout the country. The groups are limited to less than 20 people, making possible all-important personal attention. Contact the Grantsmanship Center at Box 44759, Los Angeles, Calif. 90044, for current details and fees.

The Foundation Center, headquartered in New York City, began offering low-cost seminars in 1980 with the assistance of a grant from McDonalds Corporation. The center provides a series of 30 seminars in various cities to help nonprofit organization managers develop such vital skills as research for funding, proposal writing, and program planning. The grant will enable the center to sponsor full-day seminars for 100 people in each of the 30 cities for about $10 per person. The sessions will be hosted by the center's regional libraries in each city (see Appendix 1). The libraries have all the publications of the Foundation Center, as well as Internal Revenue Service (IRS) returns—an especially useful tool in studying foundations. These seminars are designed to provide an intensive, low-cost educational program that may eventually be offered on a continuing basis in cities across the country. Center officials expect that the project will strengthen the services offered by the branches at the same time that it helps the grant seekers.

For the date of the seminar in the nearest city, call 800-424-9836. Additional information on the program may be obtained from the Director of Public Services, The Foundation Center, 888 Seventh Ave., New York, N.Y. 10019.

The Library and the Law

The grants coordinator must be aware of the library's status in two important legal areas: adherence to civil rights requirements and possible involvement with copyrights and patents.

CIVIL RIGHTS REQUIREMENTS

Every applicant for federal funds must adhere to the provisions of the Civil Rights Act of 1964, which states that no person shall be excluded from participation in, denied the benefits of, or be subjected to discrimination on the ground of race, color, or national origin under any program or activity receiving federal financial assistance. Grantee institutions are required to file Assurance of Compliance according to the guidelines of each granting agency. This can be done on a "blanket" basis for all activities for which an agency's support may be sought. The grants coordinator should determine whether the library's parent institution has made such filings and should get copies of them for the agencies of greatest interest to the library. If the institution has not filed an Assurance of Compliance with one or more agencies, this should be done on the initiative of the grants coordinator.

Many federal programs require assurance that institutions have filed Affirmative Action Plans. Such plans assure that positive, systematic efforts are being made to provide opportunities to minority groups. The grants coordinator should obtain a copy of the institution's Affirmative Action Plan and should determine when it was filed and when it was accepted. If the institution has no such plan, the coordinator should discuss the issue with the appropriate administrative personnel of the library and the parent organization. However, the actual preparation and submission of such a plan, which is a major undertaking, should not be within the grants coordinator's authority.

COPYRIGHTS, PATENTS, TITLES TO EQUIPMENT

The reports, data bases, or other materials produced under a grant may often be copyrighted.* The grants coordinator should determine the organization's policy in such matters. Is the copyright to belong to the individual or the institution? The common practice is for the institution to hold the copyright for work produced using the organization's time and facilities. There is seldom a great deal of royalty income at stake, but some difficult political situations have developed from a lack of clarity of policy.

Foundations and corporations seldom establish any requirements in this regard. Federal agencies generally follow the policy that materials produced with the support of public funds must be placed in the public domain.

Libraries are not often involved with patents, but at least two libraries

---

*For information on grants and the Copyright Act of 1976, known as the new copyright law, see Donald F. Johnston, *Copyright Handbook* (New York: R. R. Bowker Co., 1978), pp. 55, 56.

have in recent times had difficulties concerning staff members who patented processes developed with grant funds. Although foundations seldom incorporate patent clauses in their grant awards, corporations and federal agencies often do so. Corporations usually seek to share in a patent, while federal agencies prefer to assign patents to a nonprofit organization.

One university in the South was embroiled in a legal battle with a faculty member who developed and patented a product on university time with federal funds. Since the federal agency had not stipulated who would hold the patent rights and the university had no covering policy, legal action was the only recourse. However, after the legal expenses began to mount, the parties settled out of court. The income-sharing agreement reached in this case has influenced the development of policies in institutions of higher education. Policies usually provide for a percentage split, with the institution's share increasing as the income rises.

Any project that involves the acquisition of equipment with a useful life longer than the duration of the project can be troublesome if the grant or contract does not clearly state where the title to the equipment is to vest when the project is concluded. Foundations usually leave the matter up to the institution that requested the funds. It should be noted, however, that foundations are extremely reluctant to fund equipment costing more than a few hundred dollars unless that is the principal purpose of the grant.

Federal agencies usually stipulate that the title shall vest in the institution, although a few agencies retain title so that they may reassign the equipment. Some federal agencies assist grantees in obtaining "surplus" or "excess" property. Surplus property is offered by the General Services Administration (GSA). Excess property has been determined to be an agency's own property that is in excess of the requirements of that agency.

Federal agencies prefer not to fund equipment acquisitions. Normally, anything costing more than $1,000 and having a useful life of more than one year must be approved item by item. General purpose equipment, which would be useful long after the grant period is over, is rarely authorized.

Corporations usually do not provide equipment funds, but they do make contributions of equipment they manufacture. One New England library school library obtained a grant of several computer terminals from a local manufacturer, and a midwestern library received a larger number of microform readers from the company that made them.

It is the grants coordinator's task to determine institutional and funding source policies regarding equipment and to make certain that the question of title to such equipment at the end of the project is clearly stipulated in the grant or contract.

Expenses

To serve the library in the most efficient manner, the grants coordinator must be aware of and sometimes become involved in matters of tax status, direct and indirect costs involving the institution, and the implications of cost sharing or matching fund grants by federal agencies.

TAX STATUS

The grants coordinator should determine that the library has an IRS Letter of Exemption. Foundations, by law, can only fund charitable, cultural, educational, religious, and scientific activities. It can be difficult for a foundation to determine whether a potential recipient of funds is in fact engaged in an activity eligible under federal regulations. By funding only recipients with the IRS exemption letter, a foundation simplifies the determination of eligibility.

The grants coordinator's task may be as simple as obtaining a copy of the library's Letter of Exemption, or it may be necessary to initiate an application. In that case, the first step is to obtain IRS Form 1023 and IRS Publication 557 from the local IRS office or from the national office at 1111 Constitution Ave., Washington, D.C. 20224.

Since the application is not simple, it may be wise to retain the services of an attorney. Engage an attorney who has done this type of work previously, because an experienced person may be able to shorten a process that often requires from a few weeks to a few months. The fee may be $250 or more, but an attorney who belongs to the Friends of the Library may waive the fee.

Once approved, the library or parent organization is designated as a 501C3 tax-exempt organization.

DIRECT AND INDIRECT COSTS

Every activity has both direct and indirect costs. Direct costs normally include the salaries and fringe benefits of those working on that activity: supplies, equipment, travel, telephone, and so on. Indirect costs, sometimes called overhead costs, are those incurred in providing support services that are shared by other activities. These include a portion of the general administration of the organization, physical plant, utilities, custodial services, computing facilities, and the like.

The indirect cost is often included in a grant, particularly one from a government agency. The federal government authorizes the use of a predetermined indirect cost or overhead rate by nonprofit institutions. This simplifies the negotiation of a grant because that portion has already been resolved. Many institutions have already negotiated a rate that would apply to the grants that may be sought by the library. The grants coordinator should determine whether his or her institution has done so and should know what the percentage is. It is not uncommon for the rate to be 60 percent, and higher in institutions of higher education. The percentage may be based either on total direct cost or on the total of salaries and wages.

Indirect costs are treated differently even by federal agencies with very similar grant programs. For example, the National Historical Publications and Records Commission (NHPRC) does not allow federal grant funds to be allocated to cover indirect costs, although indirect costs may be included in the applicant's cost sharing. The National Endowment for the Humanities (NEH) does permit charges to grant funds for indirect costs, provided that the grantee has previously negotiated an indirect cost rate with a federal agency.

The determination of whether an item is to be included as a direct or an indirect cost is dependent on institutional policy. The grants coordinator must therefore have a clear idea of what is to be included in the direct costs that appear on the grant application. The grants coordinator is normally not involved in the indirect cost negotiation or in the administration of the funds received as compensation for indirect costs.

Most foundations and corporation grants do not include compensation for indirect costs, but some types of expenses for supporting services may be allowed as direct costs. The grants coordinator needs to understand the concept well so that he or she can accurately ascertain what a funding source will permit.

Many foundations that do not accept the concept of indirect costs will allow such budget elements as space and equipment rental even if the rental is from a parent institution. Telephone, photoduplication, and several other cost categories are acceptable if itemized, but they are unacceptable if grouped under a broad heading such as "administrative costs."

Corporations will usually make grants for specific activities for which the costs have been detailed. They often accept the concept of administrative costs for such things as the personnel office or the maintenance staff, but they seldom will contribute toward general institutional overhead.

The issue of indirect costs must be resolved with each funding source before proposals and proposal budgets are prepared. The appropriate person to contact locally is the one who must endorse the grant application. That is normally the chief fiscal officer or the director of research. The program officer of the foundation or corporation of interest to the library should also be consulted.

COST SHARING OR MATCHING

Cost sharing or matching fund grants are often made by government agencies. The applicant is expected to commit facilities, equipment, or personnel to share in the cost. This makes the agency's dollars go farther, and it may lead to greater institutional concern for the project. The match is usually no more than 50 percent or, more commonly, 1 to 10 percent. *Cost sharing* usually describes contributions in kind; *matching funds* describes an actual matching of cash.

The best-known matching fund programs are those of the National Endowment for the Arts (NEA) and NEH. The common term for these matches is *challenge grants*. They are a means by which institutions concerned with the arts or humanities may strengthen their financial situations by generating support from nonfederal sources. For every dollar awarded under the Challenge Grant program, the equivalent of at least three nonfederal matching dollars must be raised.

The grants are called "challenge grants" because they:

Challenge an institution to examine carefully both its traditional sources of support and untapped potential sources, its present audiences and others which it might usefully serve, and its long-range programming and financial needs;

Challenge members of the public to demonstrate the value they place on their local arts or humanities institutions and to express their concern about the continued functioning of those agencies;

Challenge state and local governments, business firms, labor organizations, and civic groups to recognize the role played by the arts or humanities in the educational or cultural life of their state and community and to help support that role.*

Traditional NEA and NEH grant support has been in regular program categories and for specific projects in the arts and humanities with a defined scope, duration, and result. Challenge grants, by contrast, offer institutions the assistance they need to carry out basic functions—in addition to encouraging nonfederal sources to share that support. Thus, challenge grants may be used to help in fund-raising efforts for general operating expenses, to defray deficits; to cover increased costs, renovation of facilities, acquisition of equipment and materials; for maintenance, preservation, and conservation of collections; or for other management and administrative expenses.

It is expected that most applicants will develop multiyear plans and that funds will be utilized over a two- or three-year period. The federal portion of a challenge grant may be as much as $1 million a year, depending on the merits of individual applications and the availability of funds.

For further information, write the Challenge Grants Office of NEA or NEH, Washington, D.C. 20506.

*NEH Challenge Grant brochure, n.d.

Cost sharing, on the other hand, generally is required in research-type grants and most often is prescribed by Congress in the various appropriation acts. For example, the appropriation acts for a number of agencies contain the following:

None of the funds provided in this Act may be used for payment, through grants or contracts, to recipients that do not share in the cost of conducting research resulting from proposals for projects not specifically solicited by the Government: Provided, That the extent of cost-sharing by the recipient shall reflect the mutuality of interest of the grantee or contractor and the Government in the research.*

The term *in kind* refers to noncash contributions used to meet the cost-sharing requirement. In the case of a public library, this is often donated labor. *Grantee-incurred* costs are those paid by the grantee prior to the current period, such as the purchase of space. The rental value or annual depreciation can be used as part of the library's cost participation.

A library that proposes to undertake a matching-funds or cost-sharing program involving large sums of money will need to have a fund-raising mechanism in place before it receives its first grant from the funding source. The first portion of the match must often be in hand within a year. The prospect of both designing a campaign and getting money within a single year is not good.

Foundations and corporations rarely seek to have the grantee share the cost. No general guide to cost sharing and matching funds exists, so the grants coordinator must become familiar with the practices of each funding source.

Internal staff communication about the grantsmanship process is most important. The grants coordinator will need to rely on members of the staff for ideas, proposal research and writing, and project direction when funds are obtained. It is imperative that he or she put the grantsmanship effort into perspective. It will require several months to get the first proposal out and several more to get a response. The success of the commitment to systematic fund raising usually can first be measured about two years after the program is begun.

Basic Questions and Answers

Q. Why should a library select a grants coordinator over a professional fund raiser?

A. The professional fund raiser is not usually a librarian, which may result in a proposal that lacks real substance.

*NSF brochure, n.d.

Q. What are the basic duties of a grants coordinator?

A. Learning fund-raising techniques through experience, reading, and conference attendance; identifying fund sources; establishing contacts with organizations; preparing or assisting in proposal preparations.

Q. Is there an alternative if a library cannot afford a grants coordinator?

A. Yes, a joint venture with one or more other libraries.

Q. What is the main advantage of a grantsmanship consultant?

A. As a reviewer and critic of the proposal.

Q. Where can library staff find out about grantsmanship seminars?

A. The Grantsmanship Center in Los Angeles or the Foundation Center in New York City.

Q. What is an Affirmative Action Plan?

A. A plan filed by the library or its parent institution assuring that positive, systematic efforts are being made to give opportunities to minority groups; it is required by many federal programs.

Q. Does a copyright apply to reports or other material produced under a grant?

A. Yes, very often.

Q. When work is produced under a grant, does the copyright belong to the institution or the individual?

A. Usually the institution, but this should be ascertained at the outset by the grants coordinator or staff.

Q. Do corporations provide funds for equipment?

A. Generally, no, but they may contribute equipment they manufacture.

Q. What is a Letter of Exemption?

A. An IRS form the library must file in order to be designated as a tax-exempt organization.

Q. What is cost sharing?

A. Contribution to the cost by the grant applicant in the form of use of its own facilities, equipment, or personnel.

Q. What is cost matching?

A. An actual contribution of cash by the applicant, usually no more than 50 percent, commonly 1 to 10 percent, of the total.

Q. What is a challenge grant?

A. A method by which institutions concerned with arts or humanities strengthen their financial conditions by gaining support from non-federal sources.

5
Where to Look
for Potential Fund Sources

ONCE THE GOALS and objectives of the library have been established and clearly understood, the search for funds by the grants coordinator, or other library personnel, must begin in earnest. Fortunately, there are available numerous publications, services, and foundation listings to aid the new seeker of funds.

Publications and Services

The best place to begin a search for grant funds is the *Annual Register of Grant Support,* published by Marquis Who's Who, Inc., 200 E. Ohio St., Chicago, Ill. 60611. It includes information on all kinds of funding sources—foundation, government, and corporate. Entries are arranged by fields and many cross references are supplied. Do not look under libraries alone, but also the specific topic(s) of the project(s) contemplated.

Each entry describes the areas of interest of the funding source, the types of support provided, the amount granted each year, and the maximum amount of a single grant. Also given are the annual number of applicants and the number of awards, so that one may determine the ratio of applications to awards.

Application procedures and deadlines are supplied, as well as the normal duration of grants. Use the latest edition to obtain the name of the person to whom to direct inquiries.

The Foundation Center publishes numerous grantsmanship tools and offers a broad range of services to the fund seeker. Information may be obtained from many libraries of grantsmanship tools throughout the nation, but the largest is located in the Foundation Center's headquarters (888 Seventh Ave., New York, N.Y. 10019). In addition to the type of pertinent reference materials discussed here, the library contains more than 1,500 books on foundations, many journals on foundations and fund raising, Internal Revenue Service (IRS) forms filed by foundations (see the sample instructions for ordering private foundation returns at the end of this chapter), annual reports for more than 300 foundations, and a well-qualified professional staff. A slightly smaller library is maintained by the Foundation Center at 1001 Connecticut Ave., N.W., Washington, D.C. 20036. The Donors' Forum maintains a similar comprehensive collection at 208 South La Salle St., Chicago, Ill. 60604. The Foundation Center has arranged for more than 50 additional institutions to maintain the center's basic collections, as well as some other publications. The directory for these regional centers is listed in Appendix 1.

Information on large foundations is available in the *Foundation Directory,* a publication of the Foundation Center. Over 2,800 foundations with more than $1 million each in assets or awarding more than $100,000 per year are included. The *Directory* is indexed by fields of interest, foundations by state and city, foundations by name in alphabetical order, and by names of trustees, administrators, and major donors.

Financial data in the *Foundation Directory* is usually more complete than in the *Annual Register,* including assets, income, expenditures, and the number and range in size of grants from lowest to highest amount. But the *Directory* does not tell the exact types of projects that an organization will fund. That is best determined by examining past patterns of funding. For this, the most valuable published tool is the annual volume of the *Foundation Grants Index,* also from the Foundation Center. It lists all grants of more than $5,000 made in the previous year. The *Index* usually contains more than 15,000 grants reported from nearly 400 foundations.

Foundation News is a bimonthly magazine published by the Council on Foundations, Inc., 1828 L St., Washington, D.C. 20036, for foundation professionals. Its articles provide an excellent way to keep up with trends in foundation giving. The center section of each issue is the supplement to the *Foundation Grants Index,* which reports on recent grants of more than 400 foundations—at least 15,000 grants a year with descriptions and the name of the recipient. The *Foundation Grants Index* annual volume is a compilation of all grants included in the monthly issues and is an excellent way to track past granting patterns.

The *Grantsmanship Center News* is published six times a year by the nonprofit Grantsmanship Center (1031 South Grand Ave., Los Angeles, Calif. 90015). It features how-to articles in each issue on the grantsmanship process, including excellent articles on proposal writing.

Annual reports of foundations are also good sources of information, although only about 350 organizations publish them. A foundation's recently printed report is often more comprehensive and accurate than any other available source. It is particularly useful in gaining an understanding of the foundation's philosophy and any new trends in funding. To determine whether a foundation publishes an annual report, look for the words "report published annually" following the foundation listing in *Foundation Directory*. Also useful is a pamphlet entitled *Foundation Annual Reports: What They Are and How to Use Them*, which can be obtained free of charge by writing or calling the Foundation Center. The center also sells subscriptions to a microfiche collection of all foundation annual reports.

The 225 or more largest foundations with assets of at least $7 million each and grant programs on a regional or national level are included in the *Foundation Center Source Book Profiles*. These profiles are based on original source documents such as annual reports, IRS returns, and completed questionnaires returned by the foundations to the center. Usually, the most economical way to use the *Source Book* is to visit a nearby Foundation Center collection (see Appendix 1) and make photocopies of the needed profiles.

For data on smaller foundations, consult the Foundation Center's *National Data Book*. This two-volume work supplies information on more than 20,000 foundations and is a worthwhile tool for identifying local sources. Their funding focus is usually limited to a single state and they may lack a full-time staff, but an in-person contact by a well-prepared library representative can result in a small grant. Volume 1 covers foundations alphabetically and includes information on grants paid and contact officers. Volume 2 lists foundations by state and within each state in the order of the amount granted. This volume serves as a useful index to the 990 annual reports filed in state attorneys general offices or in Foundation Center regional collections.

All private foundations, regardless of size, are required to submit tax returns to the IRS. These returns (forms IRS 990-AR and 990-PF) are available from the IRS in microfiche format. They may also be examined at one of the Foundation Center regional collections identified in Appendix 1. These returns are particularly valuable for small foundations that do not publish annual reports and are not covered by the tools previously described.

Another excellent way of identifying small local foundations is to contact the attorney general's office or justice department of one's state government for a list of all private foundations registered in the state. All states require registration of foundations headquartered in that state, and several require registration for foundations from other states that actively make grants within their boundaries. A few states will provide considerable information about the foundations for a small fee. Several large states publish state foundation directories.

The pattern of grant funding by state government agencies is very uneven. Only a few states publish a directory of funding programs, such as Florida, Maryland, Washington, and West Virginia. In most other states, the governor's office is the best source of information.

Cities rarely give grants other than federal general revenue sharing funds. The mayor's office or the municipal budget office must be contacted to determine what is available.

An excellent way of searching a state directory is to identify the groups that will most benefit from the planned program and determine whether there is an existing funding program or an agency related to those needs or interests. For example, the development of a library program to support the study of special education for the handicapped by professionals and lay people might be suitable for submission to the state agency on mental health, the agency for the physically handicapped, or for vocational education, or the department of education.

Another method of identifying state sources for funds is tó secure annual reports of federal agencies that distribute funds to state agencies. In past years, the Department of Health, Education, and Welfare (HEW) has twice a year issued a publication entitled *Financial Assistance by Geographic Area*. Listed are the name of the state and also a few local agencies to which it has distributed funds. These agencies can then be contacted to determine whether they are making subsequent grants. However, because the division of HEW into the Department of Education and the Department of Human Services may affect the way in which new federal agencies distribute information, it is a good idea to request a publication by name and add "or the publication that supercedes it."

The *Catalog of Federal Domestic Assistance* (Washington, D.C: Government Printing Office), also known as the *Cátalog* or the *CFDA,* is the most comprehensive guide to federal funding. It details the programs of more than 900 agencies and comes out once a year with two supplements, at a cost of $20. Daily updating is by the *Federal Register,* at a cost of $45. Both describe programs, eligibility requirements, application procedures, deadline dates, and other pertinent information.

The *CFDA* is the responsibility of the Office of Management and Budget (OMB). The mandate to that agency is to include information on all federal domestic assistance programs that "must be requested or applied for." OMB defines a program as having an authorizing statute and budget authority to enter into obligations resulting in the outlay of federal funds. Types of assistance in the *CFDA* include formula grants, project grants, sales, exchanges, and donations of federal property, special services, and research contracts. It does not include information about revenue sharing or solicited contracts.

The *CFDA* is helpful for looking up the ongoing programs of specific agencies. It is too voluminous and appears too infrequently to be relied upon as an alerting tool, but it does have five indexes that one should learn to use imaginatively; looking under "libraries" alone is not sufficient to identify all potential funding sources. (*Commerce Business Daily*, another federal publication, should be consulted by those seeking federal contract opportunities.)

Because the *CFDA* is a very complex tool of more than 1,000 pages, it is absolutely essential to read the introduction for instructions on its use. Following the introduction are the five indexes. The first, the Agency Program Index, lists all the programs in the *CFDA* by administering agency. Next is the Applicant Eligibility Index. Columns identify the types of applicant eligible for each program: individual, local government, nonprofit organization, state, and so on. Read down the column(s) under the correct type and determine eligibility for the appropriate programs. Consult this index after reviewing another index to determine areas of interest.

Third is the Functional Index, which includes 20 broad categories and more than 175 subcategories according to the primary purpose of the program. Fourth is the Popular Name Index, listing more than 400 programs, each by "common usage" name. One can therefore look up "CETA" without knowing that it is the Comprehensive Employment and Training Act. Last is the Subject Index, much more detailed than the Functional Index. Each of the nearly 3,000 entries has program number references similar to the other indexes.

The program descriptions make up the bulk of the *CFDA*. Each description gives legal, financial, and program information. The program's legal roots may be valuable to know in determining the underlying purposes that Congress had in mind. Quoting from the legislation can add strength to a proposal. Since the specific objectives of the program are not always given in the *CFDA*, it is necessary to make contact with the agencies of greatest interest at a very early stage in the research. Types of assistance available and definitions of the various types are listed in the *CFDA*. Uses and restrictions are quoted; eligibility requirements and application procedures are also outlined.

The *CFDA* is not completely current because much of the data is submitted before final budget appropriations are made to the agencies. One of the things to determine before committing time to proposal writing is the current legislative status of a program's appropriation. And the best way to determine that is to call the selected agency.

Another *CFDA* section lists the regulations, guidelines, and literature pertinent to the program. The names and addresses of information contacts are also provided. One of the most valuable more recent additions is a section entitled Examples of Funded Projects. It will give an idea of the types of programs the agency considers as carrying out its mission and objectives. There are a number of appendices, including one that lists the circulars needed for each program application.

Progress is currently being made in the development of an on-line *CFDA*. At present, the on-line *CFDA* is less complete than the *CFDA* and is updated only twice a year, but it does speed the searching process a great deal. Ongoing access costs approximately $75 per month through any one of several services. The best source for current information on services, rates, and sources is the Office of Federal Program Information, OMB, Washington, D.C. 20503.

Foundation Listings

One way to speed the search for patterns of grant giving to libraries is by obtaining COMSEARCH Printouts from the Foundation Center. The COMSEARCH Printout of 1979 grants, under the heading of Libraries and Information Services, lists 403 grants of $5,000 or more. The arrangement is alphabetical by state and within each state by foundation name. The recipients are named alphabetically under the foundation listings. For each grant the listing includes the name of the foundation and its location, the amount awarded, the name, city, and state of the recipient, the date of the grant, and a description of the activity funded.

There are a number of private foundations with a stated interest in libraries*:

Bacon (The Francis) Foundation (Calif.)

Bell (James F.) Foundation (Minn.)

Boinsteel Foundation (Mich.)

Braun Foundation (Calif.)

Callaway Foundation, Inc. (Ga.)

Camp (Apollos) and Bennet Humiston Trust (Ill.)

Camp Foundation (Va.)

Congdon (Edward E.) Foundation (Minn.)

Consolidated's Civic Foundation, Inc. (Wis.)

Council on Library Resources, Inc. (D.C.)

Dover Foundation, Inc. (N.C.)

Eccles (Ralph M. and Ella M.) Foundation (Pa.)

*Taken from *Bowker Annual, 1980* (New York: R. R. Bowker Co., 1980), pp. 284–285.

Eleutherian Mills-Hasley Foundation, Inc. (Del.)

Emerson (Fred L.) Foundation, Inc. (N.Y.)

Favrot Fund, The (Tex.)

Ferre (The Louis A.) Foundation (P.R.)

Foundation for Biblical Research and Preservation of Primitive Christianity, The (N.H.)

Fremont Area Foundation, The (Mich.)

Frick (Helen Clay) Foundation (Pa.)

Gebbie Foundation, Inc. (N.Y.)

Glosser (David A.) Foundation (Pa.)

Goddard (The Charles B.) Foundation (Tex.)

Grainger Foundation, Inc. (Ill.)

Grolier Foundation, Inc. (N.Y.)

Grundy Foundation (Pa.)

Harnischfeser Foundation (Wis.)

Hartz Foundation (Minn.)

Harvard-Yenching Institute (Mass.)

Heineman Foundation for Research, Educational, Charitable and Scientific Purposes, Inc. (N.Y.)

Interlake Foundation (Ill.)

Justus (Edith C.) Trust (Pa.)

Kelley (Edward Bangs) and Elze Kelley Foundation, Inc. (Mass.)

Kempner (Harris and Eliza) Fund (Tex.)

Kinney-Lindstrom Foundation (Iowa)

Knapp Foundation, Inc. (Md.)

Larsen Fund (N.Y.)

Lesher (Margaret and Irvin) Foundation (Pa.)

Lincoln National Life Foundation, Inc. (Ind.)

Longwood Foundation, Inc. (Del.)

Loutit Foundation (Mich.)

Lumpkin Foundation (Ill.)

Markey (The John C.) Charitable Fund (Ohio)

Marshall (Mattie H.) Foundation (Ga.)

Martin Foundation, Inc. (Ind.)

Milbank (The Dunleavy) Foundation, Inc. (N.Y.)

Morgan City Fund, The (La.)

Morrison Charitable Trust (N.C.)

Mudd (The Seeley G.) Fund (Calif.)

Mulford (The Clarence E.) Trust (Maine)

Munson (W. B.) Foundation (Tex.)

National Home Library Foundation (D.C.)

O'Conner (A. Lindsay and Olive B.) Foundation (N.Y.)

Ohrstrom Foundation, Inc., The (Va.)

Patterson (W. I.) Charitable Fund (Pa.)

Pforzheimer (The Carl and Lily) Foundation, Inc. (N.C.)

Piper (Minnie Stevens) Foundation (Tex.)

Pitts (William I. H. and Lula E.) Foundation (Ga.)

Price-Waterhouse Foundation (N.Y.)

Reynolds (Z. Smith) Foundation, The (N.C.)

Rhode Island Foundation (R.I.)

Sherman Foundation (Calif.)

Slemp Foundation (Va.)

Snow (The John Ben) Foundation, Inc. (N.Y.)

Sprause (The Seth) Educational and Charitable Foundation (N.Y.)

Stevens (The Abbot and Dorothy H.) Foundation (Mass.)

Temple (T.L.L.) Foundation (Tex.)

Tenzler Foundation, The (Wash.)

Walter (The Rosalind P.) Foundation (N.Y.)

Warren Memorial Foundation (Maine)

Whittenberger (Claude R. and Ethel B.) Foundation (Idaho)

Williams (John D.) Charitable Trust (Pa.)

Wilson (The H. W.) Foundation (N.Y.)

Many of the institutions that list libraries in their program statements do not make regular grants to libraries. In one two-year period, for example, nearly 90 percent of the 71 foundations identifying libraries as a concern in fact gave no grants to libraries.

Many private foundations with a history of making grants to libraries make no mention of such interest in their *Foundation Directory* listings. Major private foundations with a history of making grants to libraries are:

Astor (Vincent) Foundation

Benedum (Claude Worthington) Foundation

Biddle (Mary Duke) Foundation

Campbell (John Bulow) Foundation

Cary (Mary Flagler) Charitable Trust

Clark Foundation
Cleveland Foundation
Corning Glass Works Foundation
Council on Library Resources
Cowell (S. H.) Foundation
Davis (Arthur Vining) Foundations
Fleischmann (Max C.) Foundation
Ford Foundation
Fuld (Helene) Health Trust
Gannett (Frank E.) Newspaper Foundation
Hartford Foundation
Hayden (Charles) Foundation
Hewlett (W. R.) Foundation
Houston Endowment
Irvine (James) Foundation
Jerome Foundation
Kresge Foundation
Lilly Endowment
Mellon (Andrew W.) Foundation
Mudd (Seeley G.) Fund
Northeast Area Foundation
Penn (William) Foundation
Reynolds (Z. Smith) Foundation
Rhode Island Foundation
Rockefeller Foundation
Rubinstein (Helena) Foundation
Southern Education Foundation
Surdna Foundation
Tinker Foundation

The foundations that gave the largest amounts of money to libraries in 1979 are listed in Table 7.

Foundations such as Kresge, Mellon (Andrew W.), Council on Library Resources, Ford, Irvine (James), Moody, Hillman, and Davis (Arthur Vining) have a long history of funding libraries, yet only the Council on Library Resources (CLR) specifically mentions libraries in its program statement. The moral of the story is: Don't restrict fund-raising attention to the foundations that specifically mention libraries as one of their interests.

Table 7   Major Library Grant Makers (in Dollar Amounts)*

Name	State	Amt.	No. of Grants
Kresge Foundation	Michigan	$5,250,000	19
Mellon (Andrew W.) Foundation	New York	3,581,500	14
Heineman Foundation for Research, Education			
Charitable and Scientific Purposes	New York	3,212,688	3
Pew Memorial Trust	Pennsylvania	1,791,500	21
Rockefeller Foundation	New York	1,162,420	10
Kellogg (W. K.) Foundation	Michigan	1,503,048	4
Mudd (Seeley G.) Fund	California	1,500,000	1

*Bowker Annual, 1980 (New York: R. R. Bowler Co., 1980), p. 282.

CLR was funded in 1956 to "aid in the solution of problems of libraries generally, academic and research libraries in particular." It makes grants to individuals and organizations for research, development, and demonstration projects concerned with new techniques and methods in library operations and service. No grants are made for acquisitions or buildings. In 1978–79, CLR distributed $580,808 in 16 major grants and several small grants to individuals. There were nearly 50 formal applications, but grant giving is not competitive. The best initial approach is a phone call or letter outlining the scope and nature of the project. There are no annual deadlines except for competitive programs.

Up-to-date programs announcements for grants available from federal agencies normally appear in the *Federal Register,* in Requests for Proposals (RFPs) issued by the agency, or in a separate program announcement brochure. The *Federal Register* has a section designated Notices. The following, which appeared in the August 23, 1979, publication under the heading Department of Health, Education, and Welfare, Office of Education, Direct Grant Programs: Application Notices for Fiscal Year 1980, is a typical announcement.

13.576—Strengthening Research Library Resources

Closing date: February 15, 1980.

Applications are invited for new projects under the Strengthening Research Library Resources Program.

Authority for this program is contained in sections 231–236 of Part C of Title II of the Higher Education Act of 1965, as amended by section 107 of the Education Amendments of 1976. . . .

This program issues grants to public or private nonprofit institutions, including the library resources of institutions of higher education, independent research libraries, and State and other public libraries which serve as major research libraries as defined in § 136.04 of the regulations.

The purpose of these grants is to promote research and education of higher quality throughout the United States by providing financial aid to eligible major research libraries to help maintain and strengthen their collections, and to make these collections available to researchers and scholars beyond their primary users and to other libraries whose users have need for research materials.

Closing date for transmittal of applications. An application for a grant must be mailed or hand delivered by February 15, 1980.

Applications delivered by mail: An application sent by mail must be addressed to the U.S. Office of Education, Application Control Center, Attention: 13.576, Washington, D.C. 20202.

An applicant must show proof of mailing consisting of one of the following:

(1) A legibly dated U.S. Postal Service postmark.

(2) A legible mail receipt with the date of mailing stamped by the U.S. Postal Service.

(3) A dated shipping label, invoice, or receipt from a commercial carrier.

(4) Any other proof of mailing acceptable to the U.S. Commissioner of Education.

If an application is sent through the U.S. Postal Service, the Commissioner does not accept either of the following as proof of mailing: (1) a private metered postmark, or (2) a mail receipt that is not dated by the U.S. Postal Service.

An applicant should note that the U.S. Postal Service does not uniformly provide a dated postmark. Before relying on this method, an applicant should check with its local post office.

An applicant is encouraged to use registered or at least first class mail. Each late applicant will be notified that its application will not be considered.

Applications delivered by hand: An application that is hand delivered must be taken to the U.S. Office of Education, Application Control Center, Room 5673, Regional Office Building 3, 7th and D Streets, SW., Washington, D.C.

The Application Control Center will accept a hand-delivered application between 8:00 a.m. and 4:30 p.m. (Washington, D.C., time) daily, except Saturdays, Sundays, and Federal holidays.

An application that is hand delivered will not be accepted after 4:30 p.m. on the closing date.

Program information: In formulating proposals for new projects, potential applicants should give special attention to § 136.04, which provides a definition of what constitutes a major research library and to § 136.06, which contains specific program funding criteria and the number of points attached to each. While planning grants are not deemed eligible for consideration, a proposed project may include a planning component prior to an operational component.

Available funds: It is expected that approximately $6 million will be available for the strengthening research library resources program in fiscal year 1980.

It is estimated that these funds could support approximately 12 new projects with approximately $2.5 million and support 14 non-competing continuation projects with approximately $3.5 million. However, these estimates do not bind the U.S. Office of Education to a specific number of grants or to the amount of any grant unless that amount is otherwise specified by statute or regulations.

Application forms: Application forms and program information packages are expected to be ready for mailing by November 15, 1979. They may be obtained by writing to the Library Education and Postsecondary Resources Branch, U.S. Office of Education (Room 3622, Regional Office Building 3), 400 Maryland Avenue, SW., Washington, D.C. 20202.

Applications must be prepared and submitted in accordance with the regulations, instructions, and forms included in the program information package. The Commissioner strongly urges that the narrative portion of the application not exceed 50 pages in length. The Commissioner further urges that applicants not submit information that is not requested.

Applicable regulations: Regulations applicable to this program are:

(a) Regulations governing the Strengthening Research Library Resources Program (45 CFR Part 136); and

(b) General Provisions Regulations for Office of Education Programs (45 CFR Parts 100 and 100a).

Note.—The proposed Education Division General Administrative Regulations (EDGAR) were published in the **Federal Register** on May 4, 1979 (44 FR 26298). When EDGAR becomes effective, it will supersede the General Provisions Regulations for Office of Education Programs.

If EDGAR takes effect before grants are made under this program, those grants will be subject to the following provisions of EDGAR: Subpart A (General); Subpart E (What Conditions Must Be Met by a Grantee?); Subpart F (What Are the Administrative Responsibilities of a Grantee?) and Subpart G (What Procedures Does the Education Division Use to Get Compliance?).

Further information: For further information contact Mr. Frank A. Stevens, Chief, Library Education and Postsecondary Resources Branch, Division of Library Programs, Office of Libraries and Learning Resources, U.S. Office of Education, (Room 3622, Regional Office Building 3), 400 Maryland Avenue, SW., Washington, D.C. 20202, telephone 202-245-9530.

(20 U.S.C. 1041–1046)

Following is an example of the Internal Revenue Service form for ordering tax returns of private foundations. IRS forms 990 and 990-AR are filed each year by more than 25,000 foundations. These forms afford the grant seeker helpful data on fiscal details such as capital gains and losses and other financial matters. This form, based on 1977 returns, is the latest available and was obtained from the IRS.

Procedure for Ordering Private Foundation Returns from IRS

Forms 990-PF and 990-AR are the information returns which private foundations are required to file each year with the Internal Revenue Service. Form 990-PF provides fiscal details on receipts and expenditures, compensation of officers, capital gains or losses, and other financial matters. Form 990-AR provides information on foundation managers, assets, grants paid and/or committed for future payment. The IRS films these two forms and makes them available on aperture cards. An aperture card is a conventional tabulator card which contains a window in which microfilm is mounted. You may view aperture cards at libraries operated by The Foundation Center or its regional cooperating collections. You may also order aperture cards by state (see price list below) or on individual foundations from the IRS.

To order aperture cards or paper photocopies of 990-PF and 990-AR forms from the Internal Revenue Service, address your request to: Internal Revenue Service Center, Box 187, Cornwells Heights, Penn. 19020.

If you wish to order aperture cards or paper photocopies of IRS forms for specific foundations, you should include the following information in your order: full name of foundation, city and state in which it is located, the year of the return desired, and, if available, the Employer Identification Number (EIN). This last item (EIN) will facilitate the filling of your order. If you have access to prior year records, it may be found at the top of page 1 of Form 990-PF or page 2 of the 990-AR.

The cost for aperture cards is $1.00 for the first card and 13¢ for each additional card included in the order regardless of the number of foundations requested. The charge for paper copies is $1.00 for the first page and 10¢ per page thereafter. Note, however, that aperture cards may contain up to 15 pages each, while the paper copy charge is on a per page basis.

A bill will be submitted with the order when filled. Allow four to six weeks for processing and filling the order, depending on its size.

IRS Aperture Card Price List by State for 1977 Returns

State	Price	State	Price
Alabama	$50.00	Montana	$17.00
Alaska	3.00	Nebraska	48.00
Arizona	45.00	Nevada	12.00
Arkansas	39.00	New Hampshire	71.00
California	697.00	New Jersey	219.00
Colorado	78.00	New Mexico	12.00
Connecticut	222.00	New York	1,628.00
Delaware	48.00	North Carolina	141.00
District of Columbia	87.00	North Dakota	15.00
Florida	209.00	Ohio	397.00
Georgia	146.00	Oklahoma	57.00
Hawaii	29.00	Oregon	75.00
Idaho	15.00	Pennsylvania	474.00
Illinois	489.00	Rhode Island	46.00
Indiana	151.00	South Carolina	49.00
Iowa	85.00	South Dakota	11.00
Kansas	66.00	Tennessee	81.00
Kentucky	50.00	Texas	354.00
Louisiana	66.00	Utah	40.00
Maine	47.00	Vermont	25.00
Maryland	124.00	Virginia	117.00
Massachusetts	510.00	Washington	106.00
Michigan	240.00	West Virginia	27.00
Minnesota	180.00	Wisconsin	224.00
Mississippi	26.00	Wyoming	10.00
Missouri	189.00	All Other (U.S. Territories and Foreign)	25.00

Basic Questions and Answers

Q. What major publication tools are available to library staff to begin a search for grant funds?

A. *Annual Register of Grant Support, Foundation Directory, Foundation Grants Index, Foundation News, Grantsmanship Center News.*

Q. What is a good source of data on large foundations?

A. *Foundation Center Source Book Profiles.*

Q. What is a good source of data on small foundations?

A. *National Data Book.*

Q. Are private foundations required to file income tax returns?

A. Yes, all of them regardless of size; on forms IRS 990-AR and 990-PF.

Q. Why are tax forms of interest to those seeking grant funds?

A. They provide added data, especially for small foundations that do not publish annual reports and are not covered in the major publications.

Q. Where can library staff examine a foundation's income tax return?
A. At a regional collection of the Foundation Center (see Appendix 1).

Q. What is the best information source on federal funding?
A. The *Catalog of Federal Domestic Assistance (CFDA)*.

Q. What is a COMSEARCH Printout?
A. A publication of the Foundation Center that speeds the search for grant-giving patterns.

Q. Do some foundations state an interest in libraries?
A. Yes; they are so identified in the *Foundation Directory*. However, many foundations that do not state an interest in libraries do, in fact, give money to libraries. A search of past giving patterns will locate such organizations.

Q. Where can one locate up-to-date program announcements for grants from federal agencies?
A. In the *Federal Register*, Requests for Proposals (see Chapter 6) issued by the particular agency, or a separate program announcement brochure.

6
Requesting
the Proposal

MUCH FEDERAL money is disbursed after a process that begins with a Request for Proposal (RFP), which is a document that solicits applications. RFPs are sent to those on an agency's mailing list and to those who ask for them after a public announcement of availability. An RFP typically includes:

1. A statement of the required work
2. The schedule to be met
3. Provisions to be included in the contracts
4. Criteria to be used to evaluate applications

The RFP is most commonly used for research grants and contracts. Other federal agencies normally publicize through program announcements.

Program announcements of the various federal agencies are usually issued at least once a year in separate brochures available from the agencies. (See Appendix 4 for addresses of the federal agencies that are the principal sources of funds for the libraries.) The contents (below) from a program announcement by the National Historical Publications and Records Commission (NHPRC) indicates the type of information usually included.

   I. General Information
      A. Purpose of the Commission
      B. Programs of the Commission
  II. National Historical Publications Program
      A. Scope and Purpose

B. Grants Included in the Program
  1. Book Editions
  2. Microform Publications Projects
  3. Types of Grants
     a. Outright Grants
     b. Matching Grants
     c. Combined Grants
C. Grant Applications
  1. Who May Apply
  2. Where to Apply
  3. When to Apply
  4. Applications Requirements
D. Grant Administration Responsibilities
  1. Grant Instrument
  2. Grant Period and Payments
  3. Adherence to Original Budget Estimates
  4. Grant Reports
  5. Safety Precautions
  6. Acknowledgments
  7. Revocation of Grants
  8. Records, Accounts, Practices, and Audits
E. Publication Subvention Grants
  1. General
  2. How to Apply
  3. Administration
F. National Historical Publications and Records Commission: Locator
  1. Current Members
  2. Publications Program Staff
  3. Research Staff

Federal Programs

Until the division of the Department of Health, Education, and Welfare (HEW) in 1980, HEW distributed more than half of all federal nonmilitary grants. Despite expected changes now that HEW has become the Department of Education and the Department of Human Services, it is worthwhile to understand HEW procedures used over the years. Once that complex structure is understood, other federal grant programs become easier to master.

The Education Amendments of 1974 (P.L. 93-380) established the Office of Libraries and Learning Resources in what was then the Office of Education. It administers all programs related to libraries and information centers and educational technology. It has a responsibility to:

Improve public library services;

Stimulate interlibrary cooperative activities;

Provide school library resources and instructional equipment to public and private elementary and secondary school students and teachers;

Provide college library resources and instructional equipment;

Aid in the training of library personnel;

Assist State, local and Federal Government agencies and officials, librarians and information scientists, library educators, professional associations, citizen groups, and others in their efforts to develop and disseminate successful library practices;

Assist major research libraries in maintaining and strengthening their research collections and in making them available to other libraries and users;

Support the application of validated instructional techniques, including educational television and radio programming; and

Provide matching grants for the acquisition and installation of electronic equipment to be used in noncommercial educational broadcasting stations.*

The largest program administered by the office is Title IVB of the Elementary and Secondary Education Act (P. L. 93-380). The program, commonly known as Libraries and Learning Resources, provides grants to states on a formula basis for the acquisition of school library resources, textbooks, instructional equipment, and minor remodeling to facilitate the use of such equipment. There is considerable local discretion in the allocation of funds among authorized types of programs. In the 1980 fiscal year, $171 million was appropriated, up only $4 million from 1978.

The other large program is Title I of the Library Services and Construction Act (P. L. 84-597), of LSCA as amended. Grants are made to the states, Washington, D.C., and Puerto Rico on a formula basis. Each submits a basic plan for approval and subsequent annual program plans. The activities normally included in these plans and approved are:

Promotion of development of public library services in areas with inadequate or no such service.

Strengthening services to the disadvantaged, disabled, institutionalized, or non-English speaking.

Strengthening metropolitan libraries to serve as national and regional resource centers.

---

*U.S. Department of Health, Education, and Welfare, "Office of Libraries and Learning Resources" (undated pamphlet), p. 1.

The appropriation in the 1980 fiscal year was just under $63 million and the matching requirement of 34 to 66 percent provided approximately that much more.

Title III of LSCA is entitled Interlibrary Cooperation. This program is also operated under approved state plans. Funds are provided for establishing and maintaining cooperative activities among types of libraries at the local, regional, state, or interstate levels. Funds may be used for equipment and services, but not for construction or library materials. In the 1980 fiscal year, over $5 million was appropriated

HEA, or the Higher Education Act (P. L. 89-329), is also administered by the office. Title IIA is known as College Library Resources. The purpose of this program is to provide support to institutions of higher education for the acquisition of library resources, including binding and nonprint materials. Basic grants up to $5,000 go to all eligible applicants. Remaining money is distributed in the form of supplementary and special-purpose grants, the latter involving a 25 percent matching requirement. Since the late 1970s, the appropriation has been just under $10 million per year, but in 1980 it dropped to $5 million.

Another title of HEA, Title IIB, provides for Library Research and Demonstration and Library Career Training. Under the first program the office supports studies and demonstrations of improved service (particularly to groups with special needs), institutional cooperation, improvement in methods and procedures, and improvement of library education. Since the late 1970s, $1 million per year has been appropriated. The second program supports the training of professionals and paraprofessionals in library and information sciences. Grants are made not only for fellowships and traineeships, but also for short- and long-term training institutes for library staff. Approximately $1.5 million was appropriated in the 1980 fiscal year. The program priorities increase the opportunities of minority groups for training and provide training for people already in the library and information science fields to upgrade and update their competencies.

Title IIC of HEA is entitled Strengthening Major Research Libraries. Beginning in 1978, the program provided for grants to major research libraries to assist in strengthening their research collections and in making the collections available to other libraries. The appropriation for the 1980 fiscal year was $6 million. Most of the grants awarded were for more than $200,000 each, so that many applicants could not be funded. However, many eligible libraries did not apply.

The office also administers other programs entitled Undergraduate Instructional Equipment, Educational Television and Radio Programming, and Educational Broadcasting Facilities.

The Division of Information Science and Technology of the National

Science Foundation (NSF) is particularly responsive to research proposals that seek to increase the understanding of the properties and structure of information and information transfer or seek to contribute to the store of scientific and technical knowledge that can be applied in the design of information systems.

The division was established in March 1978. Its budget for fiscal year 1979 was $4.5 million, and the planned distribution was approximately equal among four program elements: (1) standards and measures, (2) structure of information, (3) behavioral aspects of information transfer, and (4) infometrics, or simulation models of information.

For those not oriented toward statistical measurement, the National Endowment for the Humanities (NEH) is a more suitable funding source. NEH is an independent grant-making agency that supports projects of research, education, and public activity in the humanities and closely related social science areas. The Division of Research grants support research collections, preparation of research tools, and editing, translating, and publication of signficant humanistic texts. The Division of Public Programs seeks to encourage broad public understanding and appreciation of the humanities through projects involving libraries, museums, and broadcast media. The Division of Special Programs encourages experimental programs and thematic programs of broad interest. It offers challenge grants to stimulate increased support for humanistic institutions, including libraries. (See the explanation of challenge grants in Chapter 4 under Cost Sharing or Matching.) Grants are not made in support of specific "project" activity, but rather to support long-range, fund-raising goals.

NHPRC of the National Archives will not accept applications to duplicate materials already accessible in the United States, but NEH will fund microfilming of research materials in overseas repositories. NHPRC has two programs of interest to libraries: a national historical publications program ensures the dissemination and more general availability of documentary source material important to the study of American history, and a records program assures the preservation of historical records, provides guides to historical records in repositories in the United States, training of archivists and others, arrangement and processing of historical records, and improvement of techniques of records programs. The publications program supports the collecting, compiling, editing, and publication of papers or documents of national importance. Both printing and microfilming projects are supported. In 1978 only seven new projects were funded because most of the $2.2 million available went to ongoing projects previously approved. The records program committed $1.3 million in 1978 to a number of manuals, directories, and bibliographic tools. This program also includes funds for fumigation, cleaning, rebinding, repair, lamination, and other forms of preservation of manuscript materials. The 1980 appropriation rose to $4 million, thus allowing an expansion in the programs of the NHPRC.

The National Endowment for the Arts (NEA) is an independent agency of the federal government similar to NEH. Very few libraries have applied for NEA grants, but grant opportunities do exist. The Visual Arts Program, for example, provides funds to enable cities, universities, and other nonprofit groups to commission or purchase works of art for public places. It also helps organizations organize or borrow photographic exhibitions. The Special Projects Program is a potential source for projects involving the development of bibliographies or the microfilming of unique collections of library materials or architecture and planning, dance, music, and the other arts supported by NEA. Approximately $150 million was available in 1980. (A number of other federal agencies have funded library grants; see Appendix 4.)

Corporation Policies

Corporations tend to give only in or near the communities where they have plants or offices. The best way to begin a search for corporate donors is to determine whether any of the corporations with a history of giving to education are located in or near one's community. Grants to libraries are generally included under the broad rubric of education. Simply looking up in the local telephone directory the list of names that follows will help to create a starting point. Details can then be obtained by consulting the *Double 500 Directory* and the *Million Dollar Directory*.

Keep in mind that financially healthy corporations tend to be generous in giving money, but corporate policy regarding giving is an even more critical factor. Ideally, the first contact should be made locally with a key executive in the target company. The contact person, perhaps a business executive acting on behalf of the library, might arrange a luncheon meeting to discuss the project concept.

The following major corporations have a history of giving to education: (Contact the company's local office to determine current interests.)

Aerospace Corp.
Allied Van Lines, Inc.
Aluminum Co. of American (Alcoa)
American Airlines
American Cyanamid Co.
Arizona Public Service Co.
Avon Products
Bank of America

Bell Telephone Co. of Pennsylvania
Borden, Inc.
C & P Telephone Co. (Virginia)
Carson Pirie Scott & Co.
Chase Manhattan Bank
Chrysler Corp.
Citizens & Southern National Bank
Consolidated Edison Co. of New York, Inc.
Continental Illinois National Bank & Trust Co.
Crown Zellerbach Corp.
Deere & Co.
Eastman Kodak Co.
Equitable of Iowa
Exxon Corp.
Firestone Tire & Rubber Co.
First Pennsylvania Bank
General Electric Co.
General Foods Corp.
General Mills, Inc.
Girard Bank
B. F. Goodrich Co.
INA Corp.
Interlake, Inc.
International Paper Co.
International Telephone & Telegraph Corp.
John Hancock Mutual Life Insurance Co.
Kaiser Industries Corp.
Kimberly-Clark Corp.
Lever Brothers Corp.
Eli Lilly & Co.
Metropolitan Life Insurance Co.
Michigan Bell Telephone Co.
Morgan Guaranty Trust Co. of New York
Motorola, Inc.
Mountain Bell Telephone Co.
New York Telephone Co.
Northrop Corp.

Norton Co.
Ohio Bell Telephone Co.
Olin Corp.
Pet, Inc.
Pfizer, Inc.
Philadelphia Electric Co.
Philadelphia National Bank
Philip Morris, Inc.
Rohm & Haas Co.
Shell Oil Co.
SmithKline Corp.
Sonesta Hotels
Southwestern Bell
E. R. Squibb & Sons
Travelers Insurance Co.
TRW, Inc.
Union Carbide Corp.
United California Bank
United States Steel Corp.
United States Trust Co. of New York
United Telecommunications, Inc.
Western Electric Co.
Western Massachusetts Electric Co.
Xerox Corp.

Basic Questions and Answers

Q. What is a Request for Proposal (RFP)?
A. A document that solicits applications for federal money usually for research.

Q. How often do federal agencies issue announcements of programs?
A. Usually at least once a year.

Q. Where are the programs announced?
A. Usually in the agency brochures, available from the particular agency.

Q. What is the best way to begin a search for corporate funds?
A. Consult the telephone book for corporations in your area; obtain details from *Double 500 Directory* and *Million Dollar Directory*.

7

Contacting
Funding Sources

AFTER BUILDING a list of possible foundations, government agencies, and corporations, the grant seeker must build a list of contacts within each funding source. This can be done by consulting the reference tools described in Chapter 5 or by calling the various sources and asking for the name or names of key people to contact.

Initial Application

Once a contact is known, the next step is normally the preparation of a letter to explain the proposed project and to solicit information on whether the funding source might support it. One reason that letters get a large number of negative answers is because the writer cannot determine when lack of understanding rather than lack of interest causes someone to say no. In-person and telephone contacts, on the other hand, are truly interactive. What is not understood can be explained and the proposed program can be described from a different perspective to increase understanding or stimulate interest.

There are a number of advantages to making the initial contact with the funding source by telephone. It establishes personal contact; it can produce an immediate answer as to the availability of funds and the funding source's probable level of interest in the type of project the library administration has in mind; and it can set a meeting time with the program officer. The chief disadvantages are that the person at the other end may ask tough questions. This can be an asset for someone who is well prepared and poised, but can be disastrous for others. There is no universally valid technique, but the value of the telephone approach has been demonstrated by many expert grant seekers.

For those who dislike or perform poorly on the telephone, a meeting can be arranged by letter. The letter should briefly describe the project and the amount and duration of funding sought, and ask for an appointment of up to 30 minutes for the preferred date. Include at least one alternate date.

Dealing with a foundation or corporation is usually less formal than dealing with a government agency. Most information can be obtained on a visit or by a phone call. It is, however, a good idea to send the follow-up letter as a thank you and to summarize the discussion.

Another good idea is to develop an abstract of the proposal, preferably from one to five pages in length. Leave it with those who express an interest. It should spell out the need, emphasizing the importance of the problem, the unique ability of the proposing institution to address it, and the significance of the project for other libraries or the broader community.

Library staff should know the type of funding being sought, because as a whole, funding sources shy away from giving certain types of support, among them:

1. General operating expenses
2. Building and other construction projects
3. Maintenance of existing projects
4. Emergency or bail-out funding

There are exceptions, of course. Several foundations and government agencies provide construction grants, especially when these are matched with local funds. If construction funds are sought, it is important to determine which funding sources will consider such applications.

When seeking operating, maintenance, or emergency funding, it is essential to demonstrate the special significance of the program and that the support is temporary. No funding source wants to be responsible for supporting a grantee year after year, nor does it want responsibility for the failure of a grantee because support has been discontinued.

In any first contact with a funding source, one is seeking to:

1. Ascertain that the program is within the scope of the funding source's activity
2. Determine whether there might be funds available
3. Lay the basis for an ongoing relationship so that the funding source will keep the library on its mailing list and will be responsive in the future to additional contacts

If the initial contact with the funding source reveals that a proposed program is of interest and that money is, in fact, available to fund new proposals, library staff should identify the other information that should be in the proposal and determine the appropriate format and the timeable for preparation and submission. Most of this information can be obtained in a few minutes. It is often summarized in writing, and the instructions are usually very brief and simple.

The amount of information needed for application to a federal or state agency is usually much greater. Among the questions that must be raised are:

Correct name of the grant program

How and where the program announcement is issued—*Federal Register,* Request for Proposal (RFP), program announcement brochure

Amount of money actually expected to be available for new grants

Objectives of the legislation under which the grant program was established

Regulations developed for the program

Who actually administers the program

Who will review the proposals and with what guidelines

Any geographic or other criteria in categorizing proposals

Format of the proposal

Need for special forms to accompany the proposal

Requirement for submission of a letter of interest prior to the submission of a proposal

Application deadline

Expected proposal review and grant award dates

Average size of grants to be awarded

Restrictions placed on the use of funds

Matching requirements

List of past grants awarded

Copies of proposals previously funded

The agency must respond to requests for information of this type. It is not realistic to expect answers to all questions over the telephone or on a first visit. A follow-up letter to a telephone call or visit is an excellent way of formally establishing the request. A sample of a typical letter follows; the legislation and the proposal are fictional. Note that the writer recalls what has been provided. as well as stating the remaining information needs.

Dear_____:

Thank you for talking with me yesterday. I'm pleased that Congress has funded Title XC of the Higher Education Act and that you have developed the regulations for the distribution of funds. We are interested in conducting a project to organize the archives of the Civil Liberties League and make these valuable research materials available to scholars and lay persons around the nation, especially as the league's fiftieth anniversary approaches and it has decided to reaffirm the principles of its original charter.

We expect that the project will take two years to complete if we are able to start by October 1, 1982. We expect to spend $200,000, of which half will be committed to the calendaring of the vast collections of materials associated with the league's efforts to protect the rights of native Americans. This collection has only recently been restored after it was flood-damaged at the league's headquarters.

We apparently agreed when we talked that the objectives of the legislation establishing your program encompass what we are seeking to do. If you have confirmed that, please send me the application forms for the March 1, 1982, deadline as well as a copy of the regulations and priorities you have established. You indicated that the average award would be in the $100,000 to $200,000 range. Is that a one-year award? Will some of your money be set aside next year for continuation awards or will we have to compete again if we are funded this year? We have confirmed that our institution will match the grant with space, equipment, and supplies. That is acceptable, is it not?

You said that awards would be evaluated by a panel of professional librarians and ranked by geographic areas. Please tell us which states will be included in the region to which we have been assigned.

The letter of intent will go out next week as you suggested. We will enclose a descriptive brochure about our library and a brief description of the Civil Liberties League Collection.

Thanks for all your help. Do keep us on your mailing list.

Cordially,

(Name)
(Title)
(Telephone number, if not on letterhead)

As already noted, almost all of the larger foundations publish annual reports for public distribution. They often contain lists of recent grants as well as other information of value to potential grant applicants. A letter to the foundation will usually place a library on the mailing list. Interviews with program officers at federal agencies reveal that few prospective applicants ever inquire about the agency's mission and goals. This is a serious mistake, because missions and goals are taken seriously by the program staff. Each federal agency has a statement of its mission and goals. The mission is usually set forth in the legislation establishing the agency. It is important to determine the mission because it sets the parameters for funding activities.

For example, the mission of the National Institute of Education (NIE) is to support the policy of the United States to provide every person an equal opportunity to receive an education of high quality regardless of race, color, religion, sex, national origin, or social class. The agency has elaborated on its mission by setting forth the following goals:

1. Helping to solve or to alleviate the problems of and promote the reform and renewal of American education.
2. Advancing the practice of education, as an art, science, and profession.
3. Strengthening the scientific and technological foundations of education.
4. Building an effective educational research and development system.

NIE appears to have placed a heavy emphasis on research methodology in spelling out the goals it has established for achieving its mission. That is borne out by NIE practices of the past few years. Over 95 percent of its grant funds are awarded through competitions based on Requests for Proposals (RFPs) or Grant Program Announcements in specific areas that have been determined by NIE, in consultation with advisory panels of leading educators, to be important in addressing the problems of education. The solicitations stress the importance of research methodology and the previous research productivity of the principal investigator.

Third Party Influence

One of the reasons a small number of libraries are so successful in fund raising is that they have circles of influential friends supporting them. They seek to identify individuals who can provide introductions to key people at foundations and government agencies. Influential friends cannot collect grants for the library, but they can expedite the process of information gathering and they can help to establish the library's credibility in the eyes of the funding source.

If the current board or friend's organization has not influential persons, consider reorganizing it to bring such people into the group. It is also highly desirable to maintain contact with the congressional delegation from the library's district and state. Again, such people cannot obtain grants, but they can provide introductions and obtain information promptly.

How does the funding source justify the involvement of third parties? Simply put, the granting of funds is risky. A minority of the applicants are known to the funding source. There is limited staff time available to evaluate the credibility of applicants. Some people may write good proposals but lack the ability to manage a project successfully. Some applicants have excellent potential projects that may not be adequately detailed in the proposal.

The problem faced by the funding agency is particularly acute just before its deadline for awarding grants. It may have more attractive proposals than it can fund. There is often the choice of going either with a prospective grantee who has an established track record with the agency or with one that is a new applicant. It is safer to fund the "old timer," but if there are distinguished experts who are known and respected supporting the new applicant, the scales might be tipped the other way, because program officers also feel obligated to broaden the base of recipients as far as possible.

If one cannot find individuals and organizations to support the library application, there is the option of preparing a joint proposal with another organization that has an established track record with the funding source or that has already developed a strong base of third party support.

Review and Notification of Intent

Some applications for federal funds require an A-95 Clearinghouse Review. This process necessitates a review at both the local and the state levels of all applications submitted under certain programs. The review allows these government agencies to comment on programs by which they might be affected. It is essential that library staff determine whether this process will be used in an application being made for federal funds and see that key persons in the local and state agencies are contacted to tell them of the proposal before they can see it as an official document. Their questions and comments may make it possible to steer clear of possible obstacles in the review process.

The Office of Management and Budget (OMB) management circulars that apply to libraries are:

1. Circular A-102, which explains administrative requirements for grants
2. Circular 74-4, which describes direct and indirect costs and applies to grants to state and local governments

3. Circular A-110, which applies to grants to private nonprofit organizations

These circulars also include sections on grant payments, matching shares, financial management, reporting, changing budgets, and closing out a grant. Probably 90 percent of the language in the individual agency regulations is identical to these OMB guidelines, so they are basic reading. Attachment M to these circulars provides standard application forms for use by federal agencies.

In some cases, federal agencies require a Notification of Intent before a grant application is filed. This preapplication is always required for construction projects and when more than $100,000 in federal funds is requested. Agencies may, at their discretion, apply it to other programs.

The preapplication consists of four parts. The cover sheet itself requests information about the applicant and a certification by the applicant's chief executive officer and provides space for the federal grantor agency to cite its action. The back of the form provides space for remarks necessary to expand upon information related to issues that may arise during the application period. These include priority rating, clearance and review by other agencies, impact on federal land or installations, impact on the environment, and displacement of individuals, families, businesses, or farms. Part 3 of the preapplication is a general budget for the project, including total federal contribution, state contribution, applicant contribution, and other contributions, as well as the total cost. Part 4 is the program narrative statement, which, in this stage, briefly describes the need, objectives, methodology, location, and benefits expected from the proposed project. Within 45 days after a preapplication has been submitted to the federal grantor agency, the agency is to inform the applicant of the results of the review of the preapplication. If this cannot be accomplished, the agency is required to inform the applicant about the schedule for review.

A full application is usually solicited when the applicant's prospects for funding are good. However, an agency cannot deny the applicant the right to submit a full application even when it has been passed over in the preliminary review.

Basic Questions and Answers

Q. What are the advantages of an initial telephone contact when seeking funds?

A. It establishes personal contact, can give an immediate answer on availability of funds, and can set up a meeting time.

Q. What are the disadvantages to an initial telephone contact?

A. It can be difficult for one who is not fully prepared for questions from the funding source or for one who has difficulty talking on the telephone.

Q. What is a proposal abstract?

A. A paper, one to five pages long, spelling out the need for the grant and emphasizing its importance and signficance.

Q. What are the goals of an initial contact with a funding source?

A. To learn whether the proposed program is within the funding scope of the foundation or agency; to find out if funds are in fact available; to lay the basis for an ongoing relationship between funding source and library.

Q. Which funding source demands the greatest amount of data from the fund seeker?

A. The federal or state agency.

Q. What is the purpose of a follow-up letter to the initial contact?

A. To establish the request, put in writing what has already been stated, and supply any missing data.

Q. Why should a library learn about an agency's missions and goals?

A. An agency's statement of its missions and goals can set the pattern or limits for future funding activities.

Q. What is third party influence?

A. Influential friends of the library who can provide introductions to key people in foundations and agencies or help to establish library credibility with the funding source.

Q. What is an alternative for a library that does not have a third party influence?

A. Preparing a joint proposal with a library or organization that does.

Q. What is an A-95 Clearinghouse Review?

A. A process requiring a review at local and state levels for applications submitted under certain programs.

Q. What OMB circulars apply to libraries?

A. A-102, 74-4, A-110.

Q. What is a Notification of Intent?

A. A preapplication sometimes required by federal agencies; always required for requests of more then $100,000 in federal funds and always for construction projects.

8
Developing
the Proposal

Developing a grant proposal is more than just writing. It is the conscious strategy of persuading a funding source to give a positive response. The proposal must be well written, in terms of both style and substance. It should anticipate the audience. A proposal that is to be reviewed by an expert panel of professional librarians should be written differently than one that is to be evaluated by a program officer who may not have a library degree.

Write a proposal for individual people, not for an organization, because it will be read by individuals. If program officers will play a major role in the evaluation, incorporate some elements of past exchanges with them into the proposal and anticipate some of the personal concerns or interests a program officer may have. That person will probably want to reduce the risk to him- or herself, or will want to promote a program that has considerable personal appeal. One program officer at a major funding source is very enthusiastic about microforms and is usually very attracted to proposals that incorporate their use. One funded proposal was comparable in quality to several others being considered by that officer, but it proposed the free distribution of 500 microfiche copies of the study report to key professionals and libraries around the nation. The margin of difference is often that small when many good proposals compete for limited funds.

Do not set up a committee to write a grant proposal, but have the person who will direct the project write it with the assistance of the grants coordinator. If the coordinator is the better writer, have him or her rewrite the proposal so that the style is crisp, clear, and jargon-free. The entire text should flow smoothly, from need, through objectives, methodology, and so on, for those who do read the entire proposal. Highly detailed information—whether in text form, charts, or tables—should be included in an appendix to avoid breaking the flow of the main body of the proposal.

The tone of a proposal should be positive and even exciting, but it should not promise more than can reasonably be accomplished, because funding creates a legally binding contractual relationship between library and funding source. Few funding sources ever resort to legal action to compel "specific action" or performance, but they do deny future funding and—equally as bad—they share their unfortunate experiences with other funding sources.

The picture is changing, however. Several federal agencies now conduct careful audits and have demanded the return of federal funds when a grantee has not fully complied with the terms of the contract. To date, most of these cases have involved unacceptable budget administration practices. Prestigious universities have been found to be comingling funds from several grants and to be paying persons from a grant who were not included in the original application.

The grants coordinator should understand the business practices of the library or its parent institution and should determine how the funds obtained can later be shown to have been spent as specified in the application.

Forms and Instructions

It is critical that one read *all* forms and instructions provided by the funding source. This should be done with pen in hand so that each requirement can be marked and used as a checklist before the final draft of the proposal is submitted. Many government agencies reject over half of all proposals submitted for technical noncompliance before the review of content is even begun.

One of the reasons for examining previously funded proposals is that funding sources have individual preferences about the balance between conciseness and comprehensiveness. One major foundation maintains a very small staff and looks for the proposal concept. Most federal agencies have review panels that look for detailed documentation of the problem, methodology, qualifications, and so on. Several years ago, the author served on a panel that reviewed a proposal from a distinguished economist and was surprised that the group voted it down because the methodology and qualifications were poorly documented. Most of the panel knew that the economist was famous for the development of the methodology he proposed to use, but they insisted that they could not supply the missing information for someone well known when others would be evaluated solely on the basis of their proposals. The economist was subsequently funded by a foundation after reducing the length of the proposal from 50 to 15 pages.

There are foundations that do expect detailed proposals, however. Most government agencies provide detailed instructions for the preparation of proposals; most foundations and corporations do not. Nevertheless, every funding source expects a proposal to include these basic elements:

Title page

Compliance and exemption forms

Abstract

Contents

Statement of need

Objectives

Methodology

Qualifications

Dissemination

Evaluation

Budget

Appendix

TITLE PAGE

The title page normally includes the title of the project, the name of the applicant body, the name for the funding source to which application is made, and the date of the application. It is a good idea to choose a colored paper stock to make the proposal stand out from the many others the funding source will receive, but it should not be flashy.

The title should be short and descriptive of the proposed program. Attempt to tailor the title to the funding source. An organization with a particular interest in minority groups may like to see reference to minorities in a title, as an example, *An Index to North American Indian Resources*. The National Science Foundation (NSF) appears to be attracted to titles that imply scientific measurement.

COMPLIANCE AND EXEMPTION FORMS

Forms assuring compliance with the various federal statutes governing grant applicants and a statement on tax-exempt status normally follow the title page. Government applications must comply fully and carefully with the instructions provided concerning the forms used and their placement within a proposal. It is normally not necessary to include anything more than a statement of tax exemption in the case of an application made to a foundation or corporation.

Most federal agencies require that applicants use standard application forms supplied by the agency. In some cases, these are part of a standard Office of Management and Budget form (OMB Circular A-102). In other cases, the A-102 attachment M is required in addition to the agency's own form.

ABSTRACT

The abstract is a brief summary and should normally be written after the proposal. It is not an introduction. It should brief the reader as to the purpose, importance, and scope of the proposal. A number of funding sources distribute or republish the abstracts of approved projects to let others know what they are funding. The abstract must therefore stand by itself.

An abstract developed before a proposal is prepared should not be used with the final proposal unless the original concept has remained unchanged throughout the planning and investigation period. It is important that there be no conflict between the abstract and the proposal with regard to needs, objectives, methodology, budget, or other major elements of the proposal.

The abstract should be as short as possible (one or two pages) unless specific instructions have been provided, because program officers and members of review panels often do not have the time to read all proposals thoroughly. The abstract and the first few paragraphs of each section must therefore effectively present the case. The readers will turn to the rest of the text for supporting data as necessary.

CONTENTS

A contents is seldom required, but a proposal of more than 50 pages should include one so that reviewers can quickly turn to specific elements of the proposal. The contents page normally follows the abstract.

STATEMENT OF NEED

This element of the proposal must focus on a need or problem that is important, timely, and capable of being resolved. It should indicate why the particular need or problem should be of interest to the funding source. This is important not only when a proposal is submitted in an area in which the funding source has not been active, but also in an area in which it has been. Since, presumably, most competing proposals will address similar problems, the proposal must differentiate itself from others.

Funding sources are able to respond to only a small percentage of proposals, so that it is important to them that those funded benefit not only the applicants, but also a broader community. If the library proposes to calendar or catalog a distinguished collection, the statement should indicate how that collection will serve the nation or region as well as the users of that library.

Needs or problems should not be too global. It is better to define a need or problem that is limited in scope and can be met than to paint a picture of need so great that the grant will only scratch the surface.

Funding sources also prefer to support successful organizations rather than "sinking ships." It is better to say that a grant will make it possible to provide library services to the physically disabled of the inner city than to say inner city service will have to be curtailed if funds are not made available. There are exceptions to this rule. The New York Public Library in New York City has succeeded in obtaining support in response to dire warnings about its future, but it is a unique resource that almost no one is prepared to lose. Most libraries do not enjoy such a position.

The statement of need must demonstrate a sense of historical perspective. It must show how the proposed project relates to other previous and current work. It is much better to distinguish a similar project from one's own than to ignore it and have the funding source conclude that the apparent duplication is due to ignorance. A good approach is to describe the other project(s) and then say, "However, there are still several needs that remain unmet." Statistical data is very important in demonstrating a need. Avoid elaborate tables and charts, however, because proposals are usually read quickly rather than studied.

It is appropriate to underline and use subheadings to emphasize key points. Footnotes may also be used.

The statement of need answers the "why" question. Readers must be convinced of the "why" or the "how" of the methodology will not matter.

OBJECTIVES

A project will not be successful merely because it is completed on time and within the budget. It must achieve the specified objectives or outcomes identified in the proposal. Institutional objectives have been discussed previously. The objectives of the proposed program or project are closely related to the institutional objectives, but more sharply focused. One might consider them subobjectives. A library's objective may be the opening and maintenance of a specialized business branch in the downtown area; the subobjective may be the initiative of computer searching of remote machine-readable data bases if of interest to the business community.

Another way to think of program or project objectives is as outcomes.

Clear outcomes will facilitate the evaluation, which has become a common requirement of government grants and is beginning to be expected by other funding sources.

Objectives answer the "what" question. They should be clearly set forth; ideally, they will be typographically distinguished from the rest of the text. There should not be more than about six objectives. More than that number suggests poor drafting or an attempt to do too much.

One should be sure to match the objectives to the statement of needs and the evaluation. Will the accomplishment of the objectives really meet the needs? Can one determine when the objectives have been met?

METHODOLOGY

The methodology is usually the most important component of a research proposal. It describes the "how" and "when" and tells the funding source whether the applicant appears to be able to achieve the proposed outcomes. In the past, foundations have not stressed objectives as much as federal agencies have, but keen competition is making foundation program officers more critical of every element in a proposal.

There are usually several approaches to problem solving. The applicant should not only identify and describe its choice, but also explain why that choice has been selected. It is often the methodology that will be of greatest value to other libraries. The refinement of a methodology for determining and controling serials check-in costs, for example, will be of much greater value to other libraries than the actual outcome of the project at the institution that received the initial funding.

Some proposal writers prefer to call this section the "work plan." That is a particularly good choice of terminology if the project is to be divided into several phases. Is the project to include a literature search? A survey? Case studies? If so, this should be spelled out. The division of responsibility among the various staff members who will be involved should also be identified. There should be a clear statement of administrative responsibility for the project.

It is wise to anticipate potential difficulties. One library applied for funds to microfilm a special collection in a private home and had to go back to the funding source when the owner of the collection died suddenly and the widow insisted that all filming be done at the library. Travel costs were reduced, but shipping costs were dramatically increased. The application had failed to anticipate a possible change in filming location, and the procedure and budget had been made needlessly inflexible.

Another library obtained funding for a survey and committed itself to more than 2,000 telephone interviews, even though only 1,500 were necessary to achieve statistically valid results. The staff retained for the project attempted over 2,500 calls, but completed only 1,700 calls because the survey was taken during the busy Christmas shopping season. The project went over budget and failed to adhere to the methodology set forth in the proposal. It would have been better to commit to the undertaking of a survey with a sample sufficient to achieve statistically valid results with a specified minimum reliability level and the objective of a higher reliability level if possible.

QUALIFICATIONS

A granting organization wants to have confidence in those to whom it distributes money. It is therefore important that a library gather data on its past performance and current capabilities. A summary of the library's past record of administering special projects, both externally and internally funded, should be prepared. A set of resumes for key staff should also be prepared and kept up-to-date. This type of information is commonly called "boiler plate" because it may be used again and again.

It is almost solely through the resumes that reviewers judge the competency of the project director and other staff members. If a critical reading reveals serious deficiencies in the preparation of the key personnel, it is legitimate to augment the library's regular staff with outside consultants who are more expert in particular areas.

DISSEMINATION

The distribution of a final report, a summary journal article, or a workshop to train others in the techniques or skills developed during the project underwritten by the funding source is usually important to it because the source is concerned with its image. Merely offering to submit a final report for the funding source's file does not really accomplish much. A dissemination plan should be developed that reflects what one has learned about the funding source's desire for public recognition. Not only may this help in obtaining the grant, but it also lays a foundation for future approaches to the funding source.

EVALUATION

It is important that the library and the funding source be able to determine that the project has been effective, that the objectives have been achieved. Evaluation will normally go on during a project, but in a proposal the summary evaluation near the end of the project is what is expected. The evaluation recalls the objectives and determines whether they have been met. That is why it is so important that the objectives be clear.

The budget should have at least the following elements: personnel, space and utilities, equipment, supplies and printing, travel, telephone tolls, and miscellaneous. The elements should be adjusted to meet the specific requirements of the funding source and the composition of the specific budget. Any expense item that will exceed 10 percent of the total budget should normally be broken out as a separate element. For example, outside services or the use of consultants should be broken out of personnel if it will be a major element.

The personnel element is usually the largest one. Do not use current salary or wage rates; use those expected to be in effect during the project. Add the cost of fringe benefits as well, for these may be 20 percent or more of the personnel costs. It is proper to assign staff to a project for only a percentage of their time—10 percent, 50 percent, or whatever—but be prepared to show later that the person did in fact commit that time. Professional staff are usually identified by name and support staff by title and rank.

Outside services, such as those of attorneys, accountants, or consultants, should be included in the personnel category unless they represent a major component in the total budget—usually if over 10 percent of the total. If the amount of such outside services is very small, it is also appropriate to list it under miscellaneous.

These choices should be made in the light of local budget practices. The library should avoid keeping two sets of records, one for the funding source and one for its own organization.

Rent is often an appopriate budget element. A project may require the temporary rental of outside space or the assignments of space the library already has. In the latter case, an amount common to the area may be used. Check with a local realtor to determine the local rate per square foot per year. At $10 per square foot, a single office of 200 square feet is worth $2,000 per year plus utilities. These usually cost another $2 per square foot annually unless they are included in the rent. The library may choose to identify space rental and utilities as library contributed or cost sharing.

Custodial and maintenance services are usually in the institutional overhead, but if they are not they may be included here at approximately $1 per square foot annually.

Equipment includes furnishings, office equipment, and specialized library equipment. Rental is usually easier to justify than purchase unless the project is at least five years in length and the equipment is fully amortized or written off during the life of the project. Again, the library may choose to cost-share in this case.

Supplies are normally not itemized unless this element is very large or unusual supplies are required.

Travel is one of the sensitive elements in a budget. A single meeting 2,000 miles away can cost more than $1,000. That large figure looks more reasonable when broken down as $550 for airfare, $200 for four nights at a hotel, $130 for meals, $50 for ground transportation, and $70 for registration. Again, do not use current prices, but get estimates for the period of the proposed project. One librarian called an airline for current prices and put down $420 for each of six trips, only to have to pay $550 per trip six months later. A travel agent would probably have advised budgeting $460 per ticket and and quick consultation of the *New York Times Index* would have identified an article projecting a 50 percent increase in airfares.

Any project will probably involve increased local telephone service or long-distance tolls. A brief study of one university library's eight active grant projects in 1977–1978 revealed that the average project used $100 per month in telephone services. Only one of the projects actually had funds specifically earmarked for telephone expenses.

Miscellaneous expenses include all expenses that will not fit into one of the elements described. It may also include the contingency or reserve against unexpected costs. However, any figure greater than 5 percent of the project budget will probably be suspect.

APPENDIX

This portion of the proposal should include all important information that would disrupt the flow of the text if included in the main body of the proposal. Among the appropriate appendix materials are tables of statistics or charts documenting the need, letters from authorities who support the program, a detailed description of the library's resumes for each of the professionals mentioned in the qualifications section, a list of previously funded proposals with the funding sources, and anything else that will inform the reader.

Preparation

The initial draft of a proposal should be reviewed first for substance and then later for style. Keep in mind what the funding source will be seeking as the proposal is reviewed. Ted Townsend surveyed 100 foundations and government agencies to determine which were the most important factors in deciding on funding.* The top five were:

Purpose: the degree of match between interest and priorities of the funding source and the applicant

*Townsend, Ted H., "Criteria Grantors Use in Assessing Proposals," *Foundation News*, March/April, 1974, pp. 33–38.

Need: the extent to which the project addresses a significant need and the adequacy of its presentation in the proposal

Accountability: whether the applicant can be expected to implement the project successfully

Competence: the level of previous experience and preparation of project personnel and the organization's track record

Feasibility: whether the applicant has sought enough money and whether it has the facilities and people to do the job

Recent interviews have confirmed that these are still principal concerns. Ernest Allen summarized a study of 605 disapproved applications to the National Institutes of Health (NIH) back in 1959. He found that over 33 percent of all the statements lacked evidence of importance of the project. Nearly 35 percent of the methodologies were deemed unsuited for the stated objectives, and in another 29 percent the description of the approach was too nebulous to evaluate. In nearly 33 percent of the applications, the qualifications of the applicant's personnel were inadequate.[*] Discussions with program officers at several funding sources have confirmed that these are still common deficiencies, not only in health science applications, but in all types.

The completed proposal should be carefully proofread and made visually attractive. It is worthwhile to retype pages with obvious corrections or poor margins. Photocopying of the original that is to be submitted should be of the highest quality. Check one more time to make sure that there has been full compliances with all instructions.

The most unfortunate reason for failure cited by program officers at HEW, the government funding source to which most libraries turn, is careless preparation of the application. Since the late 1970s, almost 40 percent of the applications to HEW have failed for the following reasons:

1. *Inadequate planning.* Lack of contents page, section titles and subtitles in the narrative, and page numbers, making it nearly impossible for reviewers to refer each other for purposes of discussion to various sections of the application. Also in this category were omissions of important material, discussions out of logical sequence, and poorly planned budgets.

2. *Poor composition.* Examples include sentences and paragraphs so long as to be incomprehensible. Others include lack of clear intent, lack of sufficient detail, citation of meaningless references, inappropriate statistics, and purposeless lengthy digressions.

[*]Allen, Ernest M. "Why Are Research Grant Applications Disapproved?" *Science,* November 25, 1960, p. 1533.

3. *Ignoring or misunderstanding instructions.* Failure to follow the prescribed outline or ignoring prescribed sections altogether.
4. *Clerical preparation.* Inadequate margins, misspelled words, pages out of numerical sequence, missing pages; in general, sloppy, smudgy, and careless preparation to the point where the reviewers felt the project might be conducted in like manner.

Basic Questions and Answers

Q. Who should actually write the grants proposal?

A. The person who will direct the project, with the assistance of the grants coordinator; or whoever is the better writer.

Q. What are the basic elements to be included in a proposal?

A. Title page, compliance and exemption forms, abstract, contents, statement of need, objectives, methodology, qualifications, dissemination, evaluation, budget, and appendix.

Q. What are the most important factors in a funding agency's decision?

A. Purpose, need, accountability, competence, and feasibility.

Q. What is the overriding reason for rejection by a funding agency?

A. Careless preparation of the application.

9
Proposal Submission and Follow-up

MOST FUNDING sources require multiple copies of the proposal. It is a good idea to get original signatures on all copies required to be sent to the funding source. A transmittal letter is normally prepared indicating that the organization is formally making application and expressing the full support of the organization for the project team identified in the proposal.

Application deadlines are usually strictly interpreted. A postmark earlier than the deadline may not be acceptable if the funding source has specified a "receipt deadline."

Do not take chances on regular delivery by the postal service. Spend the extra amount to send the proposal express mail or by commercial courier service. It is worth the cost of $7.50 to $30.00 to meet a deadline. If there is plenty of time, use certified mail and request a return receipt so that the postal service will confirm the delivery.

Do not expect confirmation from the funding source for at least a month, and be prepared for the final decision to take six months or more. If the funding of the project within a year is very important to the library, the funds seeker may wish to submit proposals to other funding sources at about the same time, rather than waiting for a response from the first source. Grantsmanship ethics require that each potential funding source be apprised that other applications have been or will be made.

Federal agencies usually require that a self-addressed postcard be submitted with the proposal. The postcard will be returned with a processing number, which is to be used in subsequent correspondence or other contact with the agency.

Most funding sources have an initial screening to see if the proposals submitted meet the source's objectives. A library that has carefully researched the funding source and prepared a clear proposal should pass this screening.

Review Process

Proposals that pass the initial screening are given more detailed review in one of several ways:

1. Program staff employed by the funding source determine if the proposal is meritorious.
2. A panel of outside expert reviewers is assembled to review the proposals; sometimes the review is done by mail.
3. A program officer or expert consultant retained by the funding source makes a site visit to the applicant organization.
4. Portions of the proposal may be submitted to legal or fiscal experts for comment.

The comments from these evaluations are then gathered and recommendation is prepared for the top administrator(s) of the funding source. These documents are subsequently available to applicants in the case of federal funding sources.

There are usually more proposals approved for funding than the funding source can afford to support. Some kind of ranking or weighing is therefore necessary. This process is generally done in accordance with a set of criteria developed by the funding source for this purpose. Many of the suggestions for proposal writing in Chapter 8 have been based on the criteria used by funding sources.

A funding source will notify each applicant that the proposal has been approved, provisionally approved, disapproved, or deferred. Foundations and corporations usually approve or disapprove, but government funding sources usually "provisionally" approve and enter into negotiation on the project's content and budget. *Deferral,* another commonly used term in federal agencies, usually means that a project was attractive, but incomplete. It is usually held for the next round without prejudice, subject to the receipt of additional information.

Negotiation can be a different process. It should be carried out by a team rather than one individual if a considerable amount of money is at stake. The project budget director, the grants coordinator, and chief fiscal officer would normally participate.

In the case of federal grants, the review process is more formal and elaborate than that of most foundations. The decision to make or not make a grant is, nevertheless, discretionary in almost all cases except block and formula grants (see Glossary). Discretionary grants are often made after the holding of a competition. Competition for discretionary grants is of a different nature than competition for research contracts. Contracts are awarded to meet the needs of the agency. Grants, however, are awarded to assist applicants in meeting their objectives when they are consistent with those of the grant program. The purpose of competition in discretionary grants is to determine which projects are most worthy of support with the limited funds available.

Applications frequently compete against one another for support in a review that is carried out at least once a year for each program. Some programs receive applications and hold competitions on a continuing basis, and thus do not have application submission cutoff dates. Reviews normally are made under the direction of the experts in a very technical context.

Agencies usually designate a reviewing official, who is responsible for the initial processing of applications. Each application normally is given a unique identifier and entered into the agency's application control system. The original signed copy of application is placed in the applicant's official file, and an acknowledgment is sent to the applicant.

The initial processing usually includes examination of the application for:

Legal acceptability

Applicant eligibility

Authorized signatures from the applicant

Required clearances

Completeness

Conformance to administrative requirements

A number of problems may be encountered during the initial processing. Many programs establish a closing date for receipt of applications for a specific granting cycle. Many applications are received late and must be refused. Another type of problem is an application outside the scope of the announced program. Such an application must be screened to determine if it may legally be funded under a related program.

Still another type of application requiring special treatment is one that is "nonconforming"—it does not conform to all of the requirements of the published program. For example, a nonconforming application might

Contain material not permitted

Omit material required

Be made by an ineligible applicant

Be made by an applicant for whom assurances of compliance with various federal laws and tax-exempt status are not on file in the agency

Federal agencies normally make an attempt to give the applicant an opportunity to correct such deficiencies.

REVIEWERS' COMMENTS

Applications that survive the initial processing are distributed to a number of reviewers for comment. The reviews are usually done by experts in the field who are not federal employees. Each application is reviewed from the standpoint of technical merit, in conformance with the criteria specified in the program announcement or regulation. The reviewer normally considers

Need for the project

Objectives: are they consistent with or capable of achieving those of the announced program?

Proposed procedures or methods: are they capable of achieving the project objectives?

Adequacy of facilities and organizational resources

Qualifications of staff and personnel

Value or cost benefit: is the cost reasonable considering anticipated results?

COMPETITION

The competitive process differs in almost every agency. In many instances, applications compete solely for funds. In other cases, the review involves detailed comparison of not only objectives, but also methodology and qualifications.

Federal agencies usually convene panels of qualified reviewers in Washington, D.C., or arrange with groups of field readers to review applications sent to them by mail. Panels normally consist of three or more persons. Each panelist is furnished copies of the statute, regulations, and program announcements, and is asked to read and score each of several applications on the basis of the announced priorities and criteria. Written scoring instructions and forms are provided. Based on the scores given to applications, the agency prepares a list ranking them. When legal requirements stipulate geographical or other formula for distributions of funds or awards, rankings are made for each required geographic area or other category.

One particular form of competition is the so-called peer review system. Used most often for research grants, peer review uses reviewers who are the professional equals of the applicants. Peer review panels are also generally made up of persons who are not federal employees. Usually immediately following the technical review of an application, the agency performs a financial evaluation of the highest ranked applications.

COST ANALYSIS

Grant applications generally receive some form of cost analysis. Whether this review is extensive or merely an arithmetic check of the accuracy of budget figures is a matter of judgement, usually dependent on the size of the grant requested and past experience with the grantee. Any grant over $50,000 is usually given close scrutiny.

The analysis may result in a change in the amount to be awarded from that requested or it may involve the imposition of special terms and conditions to a grant to control the use of funds. Special terms or conditions are most common when the grantee is not known to the funding source.

MANAGEMENT REVIEW

In addition to a cost analysis, the funding source may review a prospective grantee's management capabilities. Elements considered in evaluating capabilities may include

Organizational structure
Past performance
Suitability of facilities
Cost control practices
Accounting policies and procedures
Procurement procedures
Personnel practices

Occasionally, there are serious questions about a prospective grantee's ability to manage a grant. There may be a lack of experience or a history of poor performance. The organization may be financially unstable or have a very high personnel turnover in key positions. The funding source may deal with such a situation by not making the grant or by awarding the grant with special conditions. In some cases the award will be contingent on the grantee retaining outside assistance in the area(s) of its weakness.

Award Process

The funding source makes a funding decision based on a review of all relevant information about the application. Applications having the highest evaluations normally are approved for award. The others are either disapproved or approved but not funded (deferred) because of insufficient funds.

Although the advice of the reviewers is generally followed, the program staff is not bound by it and makes the final decision. Reviewers generally evaluate the applications based on published criteria, but the program staff frequently consider the evolving mission, goals, and objectives of the funding agency.

On the basis of all this information and advice, the funding source makes its decision whether to award a grant. This is one of the principal functions of a program officer. Another is the "negotiation" of the grant before a final award is made. This may be used to clarify any remaining ambiguities, arrange specific budget terms, or establish any special conditions. Sometimes negotiations are used to reduce the scope and budget of a project so that it will fit within the funding source's available budget. Any cost sharing or matching is also arranged during the negotiation. Once that final decision is reached, a check is made to be sure that there are currently funds available. The grant award is then approved for payment, either as a lump sum or in installments.

The notice of a grant award itself serves a number of purposes. It formally notifies the grantee and others, it specifies the terms and conditions of the grant, and it provides a legal or formal basis for the obligation of funds. The notice should contain, among other things:

The name and identification number of the grantee

The amount of the grant

The beginning date and duration of the grant

Accounting classification numbers

The terms and conditions

Certifying officer's signature

Unsuccessful applicants for federal grants are entitled to a full explanation of the reason(s) their applications were not approved for funding. The explanation supplied may include the scores or ranking (if any) of the application. Unsuccessful applicants may also ask for an opportunity to review the evaluation forms, summary statements, and other documents.

The formal process that has been described is also common to a few very large foundations and corporations. The grants coordinator should determine whether a simple in-house review is performed or whether a highly detailed review with outside experts is undertaken so that the proposal can be drafted for the type of review it will receive.

Basic Questions and Answers

Q. How should a library send out a grants proposal?

A. By express mail or commercial courier service if the deadline is near; otherwise, certified mail, return receipt requested.

Q. How long does a funding source take to reply to a grant proposal?

A. Confirmation comes in about one month; a final decision takes six months or more.

Q. What is the review process?

A. A detailed survey by the funding source, for those who pass the initial screening, to determine if the proposal has merit.

Q. Who is a reviewing official?

A. A person in a funding agency responsible for intitial processing of grant applications.

Q. Who are grants proposal reviewers?

A. Usually independent experts in the field who make comments on proposals to the funding agency.

Q. What is a peer review system?

A. A panel of peers, used mainly for research grants, usually made up of nonfederal employees, to evaluate technical aspects of the application.

Q. What is a management review?

A. A review by the funding source of the applicant's organization, past performance, cost control and personnel practices, and other factors.

10
Grants Administration

T HE ACTIVITIES that occur after funding notification has been received are as important as the research of funding sources and the preparation of proposals. What records are to be kept? What reports must be made? When will payments be received? How may changes in the budget be made? Foundations and federal agencies all have different policies and procedures, making generalizations difficult. However, some basic data may prove helpful.

HEW Staff Manual

The staff manual of the former Department of Health, Education, and Welfare (HEW) is a good guideline for libraries that receive grants from any source. The elements required to be included in any grant notification include:*

A. State legal name of grantee and the name of the granting agency.
B. 1. State amount being awarded.
   2. If grant is awarded under the project period system, also state:
      a. Amount authorized for budget period for which current grant is made and dates of that budget period.
      b. Cumulative total of Federal funds authorized to date and the amount recommended for each subsequent budget period.

*Grants Administration Manual (Washington, D.C.: HEW, 1976) sec. 1-67-20.

83

3. If not under project period, state dates of grant period if applicable.

C. State purpose of the grant.

D. Incorporate by reference the application for the grant including amendments.

E. Cite the legislative authority and regulations under which the grant is made.

F. Incorporate by reference any Grants Administration Manual chapters or policy statements which are not incorporated into the application regulations and which are intended to be made legally binding on the grantee.

G. Include or incorporate by reference all terms, conditions or grant clauses that are required by the Department, granting agency or program policies to be incorporated into each individual grant award.

H. Include any special conditions for the grant prescribed on or with the list of approved or disapproved grant applications.

I. Include any other special terms or conditions.

J. If not clearly stated in preceding, state:
   1. Performance and financial reporting requirements applicable to the grant including the frequency and contents of reports.
   2. Prior approval requirements applicable to the grant and how approval may be obtained.

K. Name any key personnel, i.e., principal investigator or project director whose qualifications were the reason for the approval of the grant.

L. Identify the Department official or officials responsible for the administration of the grant.

M. Set forth on its face information needed for the fiscal administration of the grant, the address of the grantee and the address of its business office and the accounting classification numbers.

N. State name and address of the Federal payment office and person to be contacted in regard to payment.

O. Be signed by:
   1. Head of the agency
   2. Grants officer

A recipient of a grant from another funding source might use this guideline to seek, at the time of the award, information that will be needed at a later date.

Project Control

After determining the condition under which the grant is awarded, the library should set up a budget within the institution's regular accounting system. Account numbers should identify and track the funds. The second step is the breakdown of the budget into categories or object codes that fit both the institution's accounting system and the requirements of the funding agency. The final provision is the establishment of control procedures to assure that assets will not be misappropriated.

Although criminal misappropriation is uncommon in nonprofit institutions such as libraries, there is a high incidence of comingling funds and treating grants as part of the regular budget. An audit by the National Institute of Drug Abuse in 1976 revealed that over 90 percent of the recipients had violated terms of the grants, including:

No procurement system

No written policy for reimbursement of employee business travel expenses

No comparison of expenditures to budget

No financial statements

Use of funds budgeted for the following month to pay current monthly expenses

No systematic recording of project revenues and costs in appropriate books of records

No control records for physical assets

Delays or failure to post and close accounts*

Audits by HEW in 1979 revealed systematic violations at several major universities, most of them involving the comingling of grant funds with general operating funds.

Those responsible for grants administration, both fiscal and general management, should read Willner and Hendricks's *Grants Administration.*†

The person performing the grants supervision duties is usually called the grants administrator. It may be the same person as the grants coordinator who directed the proposal development effort, or it may be the person who administers the library's regular budget.

In general, the grants administrator's role includes being both a manager and a middle person. As a manager, the grants administrator coordinates the activities discussed in the preceding section as well as the supportive services needed to fulfill the terms of the grant agreement. As the middle person, the administrator interprets the institution's position in the grant's contract to project personnel and, in turn, their position to the institution. Willner and Hendricks referred to the grants administrator as a coordinator, but pointed out that the "authority may

---

Chronicle of Higher Education, February 28, 1977.

†William Willner and Perry B. Hendricks, Jr., *Grants Administration* (Washington, D.C.: National Graduate University, 1972).

vary but it must include control of terms and conditions of the grant and the budget and the authority to make the project work without undue red tape or restrictions."*

Summary

Despite a lessening of prospects for foundation, government, and corporate giving in the early 1980s—due to stock market declines, which caused many foundations to cut back, federal budget trimming in an effort to control inflation, and less corporate giving due to a profit squeeze—hundreds of millions of dollars were being awarded to libraries, and the most successful fund raisers appeared not to experience a decline in their levels of support.

A number of foundations—Carnegie, Ford, Andrew Mellon, and others—began to place increasing emphasis on cooperative projects among libraries and on projects that would have substantial impact on the community served by the library. The creation of a new Department of Education in 1980 also produced uncertainty. Would library programs get more or less attention in the new structure?

In a climate of change, it is particularly appropriate for a library to formalize its fund-raising procedures and to appoint a grants coordinator who displays some interest and is authorized to commit some time to become knowledgeable about grantsmanship.

Basic Questions and Answers

Q. What is a good guideline for a library seeking funds from any source?

A. The *Grants Administration Manual*, HEW.

Q. What should a library's project control system include, once the conditions under which the grant is awarded are known?

A. Account numbers to identify and track funds and a breakdown of the budget into categories that fit the library's accounting system and the requirements of the funding source.

---

*Willner and Hendricks, *Grants Administration*, p. 123.

Appendix 1

Regional Collections

Alabama
Birmingham Public Library
2020 Park Pl.
Birmingham, Ala. 35203

Auburn University
Montgomery Library
Montgomery, Ala. 36117

Alaska
University of Alaska
Anchorage Library
Anchorage, Alaska 99504

Arizona
Phoenix Public Library
12 E. McDowell Rd.
Phoenix, Ariz. 85004

Tucson Public Library
200 S. Sixth Ave.
Tucson, Ariz. 85701

Arkansas
Westark Community College Library
Fort Smith, Ark. 72913

Little Rock Public Library
700 Louisiana St.
Little Rock, Ark. 72201

California
Edward L. Doheny Memorial
Library
University of Southern California
Los Angeles, Calif. 90007

San Diego Public Library
820 E St.
San Diego, Calif. 92101

Santa Barbara Public Library
40 E. Anapamu
Santa Barbara, Calif. 93102

Note: These regional collections maintain basic collections of reference materials provided by The Foundation Center. Foundation Centers in New York, Washington, D.C., Cleveland, and San Francisco also operate reference collections. Courtesy of The Foundation Center, New York.

Colorado
Denver Public Library
1357 Broadway
Denver, Colo. 80203

Connecticut
Hartford Public Library
500 Main St.
Hartford, Conn. 06103

Delaware
Hugh Morris Library
University of Delaware
Newark, Del. 19711

Florida
Jacksonville Public Library
122 N. Ocean St.
Jacksonville, Fla. 32202

Miami-Dade Public Library
One Biscayne Blvd.
Miami, Fla. 33132

Georgia
Atlanta Public Library
Ten Pryor St., S.W.
Atlanta, Ga. 30303

Hawaii
Thomas Hale Hamilton Library
University of Hawaii
2550 The Mall
Honolulu, Hawaii 96822

Idaho
Caldwell Public Library
1010 Dearborn St.
Caldwell, Idaho 83605

Illinois
*Donors Forum of Chicago
208 S. LaSalle St.
Chicago, Ill. 60604

Sangamon State University Library
Shepherd Rd.
Springfield, Ill. 62708

Indiana
Indianapolis-Marion County Public
    Library
40 E. St. Clair St.
Indianapolis, Ind. 46204

Iowa
Public Library of Des Moines
100 Locust St.
Des Moines, Iowa 50309

Kansas
Topeka Public Library
1515 W. Tenth St.
Topeka, Kans. 66604

Kentucky
Louisville Free Public Library
Fourth and York Sts.
Louisville, Ky. 40203

Louisiana
East Baton Rouge Parish Library
120 St. Louis St.
Baton Rouge, La. 70802

New Orleans Public Library
219 Loyola Ave.
New Orleans, La. 70140

Maine
University of Southern Maine
246 Deering Ave.
Portland, Maine 04102

Maryland
Enoch Pratt Free Library
400 Cathedral St.
Baltimore, Md. 21201

Massachusetts
*Associated Foundation of Greater
    Boston
294 Washington St.
Boston, Mass. 02108

Boston Public Library
Copley Sq.
Boston, Mass. 02117

Michigan
Alpena County Library
211 N. First Ave.
Alpena, Mich. 49707

Henry Ford Centennial Library
16301 Michigan Ave.
Dearborn, Mich. 48126

Purdy Library
Wayne State University
Detroit, Mich. 48202

Michigan State University Libraries
East Lansing, Mich. 48824

University of Michigan-Flint
UM-F Library
Flint, Mich. 48503

Grand Rapids Public Library
Library Plaza
Grand Rapids, Mich. 49502

Michigan Technological University
Library
Highway U.S. 41
Houghton, Mich. 49931

Minnesota
Minneapolis Public Library
300 Nicollet Mall
Minneapolis, Minn. 55401

Mississippi
Jackson Metropolitan Library
301 N. State St.
Jackson, Miss. 39201

Missouri
*Clearinghouse for Midcontinent
Foundations
University of Missouri
52nd St. and Holmes
Kansas City, Mo. 64110

Kansas City Public Library
311 E. 12th St.
Kansas City, Mo. 64106

*Metropolitan Association for
Philanthropy, Inc.

5600 Oakland, G-324
St. Louis, Mo. 63110

Springfield-Greene County Library
397 E. Central St.
Springfield, Mo. 65801

Montana
Eastern Montana College Library
Billings, Mont. 59101

Nebraska
W. Dale Clark Library
215 S. 15th St.
Omaha, Nebr. 68102

Nevada
Clark County Library
1401 E. Flamingo Rd.
Las Vegas, Nev. 68102

Washoe County Library
301 S. Center St.
Reno, Nev. 89505

New Hampshire
*The New Hampshire Charitable
Fund
One South St.
Concord, N.H. 03301

New Jersey
New Jersey State Library
185 W. State St.
Trenton, N.J. 08625

New Mexico
New Mexico State Library
300 Don Gaspar St.
Santa Fe, N.Mex. 87501

New York
New York State Library
Empire State Plaza
Albany, N.Y. 12230

Buffalo and Erie County Public
Library

Lafayette Sq.
Buffalo, N.Y. 14203

Levittown Public Library
One Bluegrass Lane
Levittown, N.Y. 11756

Plattsburgh Public Library
15 Oak St.
Plattsburgh, N.Y. 12901

Rochester Public Library
115 South Ave.
Rochester, N.Y. 14604

Onondaga County Public Library
335 Montgomery St.
Syracuse, N.Y. 13202

North Carolina
North Carolina State Library
109 E. Jones St.
Raleigh, N.C. 27611

*The Winston-Salem Foundation
229 First Union National Bank Bldg.
Winston-Salem, N.C. 27101

North Dakota
The Library
North Dakota State University
Fargo, N.Dak. 58105

Ohio
Public Library of Cincinnati and
    Hamilton County
800 Vine St.
Cincinnati, Ohio 45202

Oklahoma
*Oklahoma City Community
    Foundation
1300 N. Broadway
Oklahoma City, Okla. 73103

Tulsa City-County Library System
400 Civic Center
Tulsa, Okla. 74103

Oregon
Library Association of Portland

801 S.W. Tenth Ave.
Portland, Oreg. 97205

Pennsylvania
The Free Library of Philadelphia
Logan Sq.
Philadelphia, Pa. 19103

Hillman Library
University of Pittsburgh
Pittsburgh, Pa. 15260

Rhode Island
Providence Public Library
150 Empire St.
Providence, R.I. 02903

South Carolina
South Carolina State Library
1500 Senate St.
Columbia, S.C. 29211

South Dakota
South Dakota State Library
322 S. Fort St.
Pierre, S.Dak. 57501

Tennessee
Memphis Public Library
1850 Peabody Ave.
Memphis, Tenn. 38104

Texas
*The Hogg Foundation for Mental
    Health
The University of Texas
Austin, Tex. 78712

Dallas Public Library
1954 Commerce St.
Dallas, Tex. 75201

*El Paso Community Foundation
El Paso National Bank Bldg.
El Paso, Tex. 79901

Houston Public Library
500 McKinney Ave.
Houston, Tex. 77002

*Funding Information Library
Minnie Stevens Piper Foundation
201 N. St. Mary's St.
San Antonio, Tex. 78205

Utah
Salt Lake City Public Library
209 E. Fifth St.
Salt Lake City, Utah 84111

Vermont
State of Vermont Department of
  Libraries
111 State St.
Montpelier, Vt. 05602

Virginia
Grants Resources Library
Hampton City Hall
Hampton, Va. 23669

Richmond Public Library
101 E. Franklin St.
Richmond, Va. 23219

Washington
Seattle Public Library
1000 Fourth Ave.
Seattle, Wash. 98104

Spokane Public Library
West 906 Main Ave.
Spokane, Wash. 99201

West Virginia
Kanawha County Public Library
123 Capitol St.
Charleston, W.Va. 25301

Wisconsin
Marquette University Memorial
  Library
1415 W. Wisconsin Ave.
Milwaukee, Wis. 53233

Wyoming
Laramie County Community College
  Library
1400 E. College Dr.
Cheyenne, Wyo. 82001

Appendix 2
Foundations

The private foundations listed in this section have a stated interest in libraries (indicated by an asterisk) or have some history of making grants to libraries. Foundation interests change so it is essential to use any listing as a preliminary screening device, not as the basis for preparing a proposal. Lists of foundations in directories may not necessarily reflect the most current funding patterns with regards to libraries; therefore, personal contact with the funding source should be made to determine the present interests of a foundation. It may be worthwhile to make note of the Council on Library Resources, Inc. (CLR), founded in 1956 to aid in the solution of problems of libraries generally and academic and research libraries in particular. It makes grants to individuals and organizations for research, development, and demonstration projects concerned with new techniques and methods in library operations and services. No grants are made for acquisitions or buildings. In 1978–1979, the Council distributed nearly $581,000 in 16 major grants and several smaller grants to individuals; there were nearly 50 formal applications. The best initial approach is a telephone call or letter outlining the nature and scope of the project. There are no annual deadlines except for a few competitive programs. For further information on foundations, the reader is referred to the sources in the Bibliography of this book.

*Amoco Foundation, Inc. 200 E. Randolph Dr., Chicago, Ill. 60601. (312) 856-6305. *Contact:* Donald E. Burney, Exec. Dir.
Provides financial aid to educational, cultural, health, social welfare, and youth organizations; special consideration given to community funds and educational institutions.

92

Appleby Foundation, The. c/o National Savings and Trust Co., Fifteenth St. and New York Ave., N.W., Washington, D.C. 20005.

Grants primarily for higher education, largely in Washington, D.C., Florida, and Georgia.

Vincent Astor Foundation, The. 405 Park Ave., New York, N.Y. 10022. (212) 758-4110.

Broad purposes; primarily confined to institutions and projects in New York City or projects significantly affecting New York City residents; support for certain cultural institutions (except programs involving the performing arts), parks and landmark preservation, and community-based programs, especially those involving or affecting children and older people.

Bacon (The Francis) Foundation, Inc. 655 N. Dartmouth Ave., Claremont, Calif. 91711. (714) 624-6305.

To promote study in science, literature, religion, history, and philosophy with special reference to the works of Francis Bacon. Grants restricted to privately operated colleges and universities in California. No grants to individuals, for building and endowment funds, or for operating budgets.

Baker (The George F.) Trust. 20 Exchange Pl., Rm. 3308, New York, N.Y. 10005. (212) 943-1441.

Broad purposes; general charitable giving, largely to institutions traditionally supported by the donor and his family in the New York City area, with emphasis on hospitals and health agencies, welfare and youth agencies, conservation, and historic preservation. No grants to individuals, for building or endowment funds, or for special projects.

Baker (The William G.) Jr. Memorial Fund. c/o Mercantile-Safe Deposit and Trust Co., Box 2257, Two Hopkins Plaza, Baltimore, Md. 21203. (301) 237-5551.

Primarily local giving, with emphasis on education and community funds. No grants to individuals.

Bell (James F.) Foundation. 10000 Highway 55 W., Suite 450, Minneapolis, Minn. 55441.

Primarily local giving, with emphasis on a local university library and cultural programs; support also for youth agencies, medical research, conservation, and hospitals.

Benedum (Claude Worthington) Foundation. 223 Fourth Ave., Pittsburgh, Pa. 15222. (412) 288-0360.

Broad variety of charitable purposes, particulary in the regional area of

Pittsburgh, southwestern Pennsylvania, and West Virginia, with a priority of concern governing its consideration of projects and programs aimed at enhancing educational and cultural opportunities for the people of West Virginia.

Biddle (The Mary Duke) Foundation. 30 Rockefeller Plaza, Suite 4300, New York, N.Y. 10020. (212) 247-3400.

Grants restricted to New York City and North Carolina, with emphasis on higher and secondary education, cultural programs, projects in the arts, hospitals, health, and rehabilitation; half of the income is committed to Duke University.

Booth Ferris Foundation. 40 Exchange Pl., New York, N.Y. 10005. (212) 269-3850.

Broad purposes; grants primarily for higher education, including that for minorities, Protestant theological seminaries, hospitals and health agencies, civic and urban programs, as well as local social agencies and programs for the performing arts. Educational grants and grants to theological seminaries and health organizations throughout the United States. However, support for urban and civic programs, social welfare, hospitals, and cultural activities centered almost entirely on New York City.

Braun Foundation. c/o Maynard J. Toll, 611 W. Sixth St., Rm. 3500, Los Angeles, Calif. 90017. (213) 570-1000.

Charitable purposes; primarily local giving, with emphasis on hospitals, elementary and secondary schools, community funds, art education, museums, and libraries.

Calloway Foundation, Inc. Box 790, 209 Broome St., LaGrange, Calif. 30241. (404) 884-7348.

Broad purposes; present program largely confined to Georgia; grants primarily for education, including buildings and equipment, elementary and secondary schools, libraries, hospitals, community funds, care for the aged, and church support.

Calloway (Fuller E.) Foundation. Box 790, 209 Broome St., LaGrange, Calif. 30241. (404) 884-7348.

Broad purposes; grants to religious and educational institutions in La-Grange and Troup counties; scholarships for Troup County students; modest gifts toward operating expenses of local community welfare agencies. No grants for endowment funds.

Camp Foundation. Franklin, Va. 23851. (804) 569-4321.

Primarily local giving with emphasis on youth agencies, hospitals, higher and secondary education, including scholarships, recreation, historic preservation, and cultural programs. Grants limited to organizations in Franklin County, Virginia, at this time.

Cary (Mary Flagler) Charitable Trust. Box 289, Millbrook, N.Y. 12545. (212) 689-8025.

Charitable purposes; primarily local giving; restricted to maintenance of family collections, conservation of natural resources (primarily environmental research and land use management), and music, including musical education and the performance of operatic and symphonic music in New York City.

*Champion International Foundation, The (formerly The Champion Paper Foundation). One Landmark Square, Stamford, Conn. 06921. (203) 357-8656. *Contact:* Thomas H. Latimer, Vice-Pres.

Primary interests are in higher education and support of the free-enterprise business environment. The foundation supports construction, endowments, operating budgets, special projects, a foundation-sponsored scholarship program, and an employee matching gifts program for educational institutions of all sizes and types. Youth agencies such as the Boy Scouts and Girl Scouts are also a special interest, as are hospitals, medical research organizations, civic and community groups, and institutions concerned with peace and international relations. The foundation also has shown an interest in cultural organizations such as museums and libraries.

Clark Foundation, The. 6116 N. Central Expressway, Suite 304, Dallas, Tex. 75206. (214) 361-7498.

Grants largely for education, including scholarships, research, and libraries, solely within Texas. Scholarship applications accepted only through the Dallas Independent School District and the Texas Interscholastic League.

Cleveland Foundation, The. 700 National City Bank Bldg., Cleveland, Ohio 44114. (216) 861-3810

The pioneer community trust, which has served as the model for most community foundations in the United States; purposes are to assist public charitable or educational institutions in Ohio; promote education and scientific research; care for the sick, aged, and helpless; improve living and working conditions; provide facilities for public recreation; promote social and domestic hygiene, sanitation, and the prevention of disease; research into the causes of ignorance, poverty, crime, and vice. Unless specified otherwise by the donor, grants are limited to the Greater Cleveland Area and are not made for capital, sectarian, or religious activities.

*Commonwealth Fund, The. One E. 75 St., New York, N.Y. 10021. (212)535-0400. *Contact*: Dr. Reginald H. Fitz, Vice Pres.

The fund's purpose has been undergoing a change in direction. In the past, a major emphasis has been on the improvement of the quality of science education offered to those preparing for careers in medicine and other health professions. Even though the foundation is repeatedly included in lists of those with a history of making grants to libraries, it has only occasionally made such grants. Unfortunately, only one grant annually can include a library on a list. It is too early to determine whether the foundation will have a greater interest in libraries in future years. Librarians may wish to tailor grant applications to reflect the demonstrated subject interests of the foundation.

Consolidated's Civic Foundation, Inc. First Ave. N., Wisconsin Rapids, Wis. 54494. (715) 422-3368.

Broad purposes; primarily local giving, with emphasis on higher education, including technological education, libraries, community funds, hospitals, and youth agencies; educational grants generally limited to private accredited four-year colleges and universities in Wisconsin. No grants to individuals.

*Corning Glass Works Foundation. Corning, N.Y. 14830. (607) 974-8489. *Contact*: Richard B. Bessey, Vice Pres. and Exec. Dir.

To improve the quality of life through support of educational, civic, cultural, health, and social service institutions. Emphasis is given to programs and communities where the company has manufacturing plants and to organizations that concern themselves with the advancement of society.

*Council on Library Resources, Inc. One Dupont Circle, Washington, D.C. 20036. (202) 296-4757. *Contact*: Warren J. Haas, Pres.

Grants only for programs that show promise of helping to provide solutions to some of the many problems that affect libraries in general and academic and research libraries in particular. The council, when appropriate, also operates programs of its own to serve the same general purpose. Attempts to support the development of solutions to problems that face libraries generally, rather than in filling localized needs. Although grants to libraries are common, the Council will also fund library-oriented organizations, individuals, and fund and administer its own projects.

Cowell (S. H.) Foundation. 350 Sansome Street, Suite 620, San Francisco, Calif. 94104. (415) 397-0285.

Grants for charitable, educational, health, and scientific purposes. Giving limited to organizations in northern California, with emphasis on programs aiding the handicapped; support also for primary and secondary private schools, and other educational programs, community organizations, youth agencies, and social rehabilitation services. No grants to individuals, for operating budgets, endowment funds, hospitals, or sectarian religious purposes. Report published annually.

Cary (Bruce L.) Foundation, Inc. c/o Richard W. Lawrence, Jr., Elizabethtown, N.Y. 12932.
Primarily local giving, with emphasis on scholarships; some support for a hospital and social and educational agencies.

Davis (The Arthur Vining) Foundations. 255 Alhambra Circle, Suite 520, Coral Gables, Fla. 33134. (305) 448-7712.
Broad purposes, support largely for private higher education, medicine, religion, and public television. No grants to individuals. Report published annually. Primary interest Florida and Pennsylvania.

Dover Foundation, Inc., The. c/o Dover Mill Co., Shelby, N.C. 28150.
Broad purposes; primarily local giving, with emphasis on higher and secondary education, church support, community funds, and a library.

Dula (Caleb C. and Julia W.) Educational and Charitable Foundation. c/o Manufacturers Hanover Trust Co., 600 Fifth Ave., New York, N.Y. 10020.
Grants to charities that the Dulas supported during their lifetime, with emphasis on higher and secondary education, hospitals, libraries, social agencies, child welfare, church support, care of the aged, animal welfare, and historic preservation, primarily in New York and Saint Louis, Missouri.

Eccles (Ralph M. and Ella M.) Foundation. First Seneca Bank and Trust Co., Oil City, Penn. 16301.
Giving limited to Clarion County, with emphasis on a library, Protestant church support, and youth activities. No grants to individuals.

Eleutherian Mills–Hagley Foundation. Box 3630, Wilmington, Delaware 19807. (302) 658-2401.
Grants-in-aid to postdoctoral scholars and doctoral candidates for study and research in residence at the Eleutherian Mills Historical Library, which has rich manuscript and imprint collections relating to French history, 1760–1820, and to American economic history, 1800–

1950, with special emphasis on business, industrial, and technological developments in the lower Delaware River Valley area.

Emerson (Fred L.) Foundation, Inc. Four South St., Box 307, Auburn, N.Y. 13021. (315) 253-9621.

Broad purposes; primarily local giving, with emphasis on higher and secondary education, including a building program, hospitals, community funds, and a library building fund; grants also for youth agencies, church support, and conservation. No grants to individuals.

*Charles Engelhard Foundation, The. 75 Claremont Rd., Box 761, Bernardsville, N.J. 07924. (201) 766-7224. *Contact*: Patricia Dunphy, Sec.

Involved in general giving programs, with emphasis on educational, cultural, medical, religious, wildlife, and conservation organizations. Grants are generally limited to organizations in New Jersey and to cultural institutions in New York City, but grants have been made throughout the northeastern United States over the past few years.

Favrot Fund. 8383 Westview Dr., Houston, Tex. 77055. (713) 467-1310.

Primarily local giving, with emphasis on advanced religious study, including a theological seminary, and higher education, including medical education; support also for a public library and population control.

Ferre (The Luis A.) Foundation, Inc. Box 4487, San Juan, P.R. 00936. (809) 764-2490.

General giving, with emphasis on higher education, including scholarships, music, and libraries; support for a local museum. No grants for building or endowment funds, operating budgets, or special projects. Grant-making program presently suspended.

*Ford Foundation, The. 320 East 43 St., New York, N.Y. 10017. (212) 573-5000. *Contact*: Howard R. Dressner, Sec.

Aims to advance the public welfare by trying to identify and contribute to the solution of problems of national and international importance. Grants are primarily to institutions for experimental, demonstration, and developmental efforts that are likely to produce significant advances within such fields as education, minority opportunities, ecology, energy, civil rights, and performing and visual arts.

Foundation for Biblical Research and Preservation of Primitive Christianity, The. Box 373, Charlestown, N.H. 03603.

Broad purposes; to establish and maintain a library of Christian books and other records available for Biblical research and study; to collect and preserve materials pertaining to Mary Baker Eddy; grants to higher educational institutions for scholarships to assist in the education of youth; to promote the cultural interests of the community.

Fremont Area Foundation, The. Box 9, Fremont, Mich. 49412. (616) 924-5350.

To benefit the people of Newaygo County; grants for youth groups, hospital, education, library, and new civic center. No grants to individuals or for endowment funds.

Frick (Helen Clay) Foundation. c/o Mellon Bank, Mellon Sq., Pittsburgh, Pa. 15230. (412) 281-3392.

Charitable purposes, including promotion of the fine arts; primarily local giving, largely for support of an art reference library in New York City; interests include Episcopal church support and church-related institutions and higher education; presently owns and operates a museum of Renaissance art in Pittsburgh. No grants to individuals.

Frost (Meshech) Testamentary Trust. c/o The Ohio National Bank, 51 N. High St., Columbus, Ohio 43215.

The Trust is set up for use in civic improvement or beautification and for the needy poor and other charitable purposes within Tiffin, Ohio, including support for a hospital, a community fund, a community swimming pool, and a rehabilitation center.

Fuld (Helene) Health Trust. c/o Marine Midland Bank, 250 Park Ave., New York, N.Y. 10017. (212) 949-6680.

Grants to state-accredited nursing schools affiliated with accredited hospitals to promote the health, education, and welfare of enrolled student nurses who are being taught to care for the sick and injured at bedside. No grants for endowment funds, operating expenses, or to individuals. Report published annually.

Gannett (Frank E.) Newspaper Foundation, Inc. Lincoln Tower, Rochester, N.Y. 14604. (716) 244-8957.

Grants primarily to educational, charitable, civic, cultural, and health institutions in areas served by the seven daily newspapers of the Gannett Group. Primary national interest is support of education for print journalism. No grants to individuals.

Gebbie Foundation, Inc. Hotel Jamestown Bldg., Rm. 308, Jamestown, N.Y. 14701. (716) 487-1062.

Grants for medical and scientific research to alleviate human suffering and ills relating to metabolic diseases of the bone; some support for higher education, hospitals, libraries, local youth agencies, and community funds. Interested in programs of preventative medicine as they relate to diseases of children, to detection of deafness, to training and education of the deaf, and to certain ophthalmological programs concerned with degenerative and metabolic diseases of the retina. Primarily interested in Chautauqua County, secondly in western New York, and in other areas only when the project is consonant with the program objectives that cannot be developed locally. No grants to individuals; grants are rarely for operating budgets.

Glosser (David A.) Foundation. 72 Messenger St., Johnstown, Penn. 15902. (814) 535-7521.

Broad purposes; primarily local giving, with emphasis on Jewish welfare funds and construction of a local library. No grants to individuals or for endowment funds.

Goddard (The Charles B.) Foundation. 5944 Luther La., Suite 1003, Box 25166, Dallas, Tex. 75225. (214) 739-2025.

Broad purposes; general giving, with emphasis on community programs and community funds; support also for youth agencies, secondary and elementary education, including a school libraries project, and a medical research institute; grants largely limited to Oklahoma and Texas. No grants to individuals or for endowment funds.

Grainger Foundation, Inc., The. 5959 W. Howard St., Chicago, Ill. 60648. (312) 647-8900.

Broad purposes; giving primarily in the Chicago area, with emphasis on hospitals, higher and secondary education, including scholarships administered by National Merit Scholarship Corporation, a library, community funds, and welfare agencies. No grants to individuals, for endowment funds, or operating budgets.

Grundy Foundation, The. 680 Radcliffe St., Box 701, Bristol, Pa. 19007. (215) 788-5460.

General purposes; grants for higher education, libraries, hospitals, child welfare and youth agencies, community funds, mental health, and community planning; support also for vocational education, the handicapped, historic preservation, and the aged. Restricted to Bucks County, Pennsylvania, and activities in which the donor was interested during his lifetime. No grants to individuals or for endowment funds.

Harnischfeger Foundation, Inc. Box 554, Milwaukee, Wis. 53217. (414) 671-4400.

Broad purposes; general giving, with emphasis on hospitals, a library, higher education, and youth agencies, primarily in Wisconsin.

Hartford Foundation for Public Giving. 45 S. Main St., West Hartford, Conn. 06107. (203) 233-4443

Grants mainly for demonstration programs and capital purposes, with emphasis on community advancement, educational institutions, youth groups, hospitals, the aging, and cultural and civic endeavors in Greater Hartford. No grants for sectarian purposes, to individuals, to organizations outside of Hartford and vicinity, for endowment funds, operating budgets except for startup costs, or tax-supported agencies.

Harvard-Yenching Institute. Two Divinity Ave., Cambridge, Mass. 02138. (617) 495-3369.

The purpose is to aid development of higher education in eastern and southern Asia; grants primarily for certain universities in Asia to support teaching, research, and study by Asians in the humanities and social sciences relating to Asian cultures; support for inter-Asian personnel exchange in these fields; sponsorship at Harvard University of fellowships for research or scholarships for graduate study by younger faculty members of selected Asian institutions; contributions to the Harvard-Yenching Library.

Hayden (Charles) Foundation. One Bankers Trust Plaza, 130 Liberty St., New York, N. Y. 10006. (212) 938-0790.

Set up to assist young people; emphasis on helping to provide physical facilities and equipment for organizations primarily concerned with youth of the New York and Boston metropolitan areas. No grants to individuals or for endowment funds or operating budgets.

Heineman Foundation for Research, Educational, Charitable and Scientific Purposes, Inc. c/o Elmer Fox, Westheimer and Co., 1211 Ave. of the Americas, New York, N.Y. 10036. (212) 425-2910.

General purposes; support for research programs in the mathematical sciences and medicine; grants, primarily in New York, also for higher education, Jewish welfare funds, specialized libraries (including the Heineman Library of Rare Books and Manuscripts on deposit at The Pierpont Morgan Library, New York), a music school, refugees, and an annual physics award.

*****Hewlett (William and Flora) Foundation, The.** (formerly The W. R. Hewlett Foundation). Two Palo Alto Sq., Suite 1010, Palo Alto, Calif. 94304. (415) 493-3665. *Contact*: Dr. Roger W. Heyns, Pres.

The Hewlett Foundation has undergone a re-evaluation of its funding priorities; the probable future areas of emphasis include arts and humanities, education (especially at the college level), population programs, and a Bay Area grants program. In the past, the foundation has made grants to the Council on Library Resources, Inc., The Foundation Center, and to the Research Libraries Group.

Houston Endowment Inc. Box 52338, Houston, Tex. 77052. (713) 223-4043.

For "the support of any charitable, educational, or religious undertaking." Grants largely for higher education (scholarships, buildings, equipment) and health care facilities (construction and equipping of hospitals), but also including some cultural and religious activities, with highest priority placed on local and state needs.

Interlake Foundation. 2015 Spring Rd., Oak Brook, Ill. 60521.

General giving, with emphasis on community funds; support also for hospitals, higher education, youth agencies, and libraries.

Irvine (The James) Foundation. Steuart St. Tower, Suite 2305, One Market Plaza, San Francisco, Calif. 94105. (415) 777-2244.

Grants limited to California, with preference given to projects in Orange County and the San Francisco Bay Area; primarily for higher education, health, youth services, and community and cultural projects not receiving government support. No grants to individuals, private secondary schools, for sectarian religious activities, normal operating expenses, or general support.

Jerome Foundation. 4020 Bandini Blvd., Los Angeles, Calif. 90023.

Primarily local giving, with emphasis on medical research, handicapped children's organizations, the blind, hospitals, and youth and health agencies.

Justus (Edith C.) Trust. c/o First Seneca Bank and Trust Co., Oil City, Pa. 16301. (814) 676-6511.

Giving limited to Venango County, Pennsylvania, with preference for Oil City; grants largely for development of two public parks and recreation areas; support also for youth agencies, community funds, and a public library. No grants to individuals or for endowment funds.

Kempner (Harris and Eliza) Fund. Box 119, Galveston, Tex. 77550. (713) 765-6671.

Broad purposes; primarily local giving, with emphasis on higher education, including scholarships and a matching gifts program, a library, community funds, Jewish welfare funds, historic preservation, medical research, mental health, and community projects. No grants to individuals.

Kinney-Lindstrom Foundation, Inc. Box 520, Mason City, Iowa 50401. (515) 424-6291.

Broad purposes; grants primarily for building funds for libraries in Iowa towns; support also for youth agencies, community funds, and education. No grants to individuals or for endowment funds or operating budgets.

Knapp Foundation, Inc., The. c/o Robert B. Vojvoda, Box O, Saint Michaels, Md. 21663. (301) 745-5660.

Grants primarily for education, with emphasis on elementary and secondary school libraries and North Carolina schools, conservation and preservation of birds and animals. No grants to individuals or for building or endowment funds.

*Kresge Foundation, The. 2401 W. Big Beaver Rd., Troy, Mich. 48084. (313) 643-9630. *Contact:* William H. Baldwin, Chairperson.

Supports a wide range of programs including challenge grants for building construction or renovation projects, major, movable capital equipment, and the purchase of real estate. Grants are almost always made to well-established, financially sound, and fully accredited institutions involved in higher education, health care, youth care, problems of the aged, conservation, and the arts. Support is not usually given for the total project costs. No support is given for operating or special projects budgets, conferences or seminars, loans, endowment, student aid, research, church building programs, debt retirement, or completed projects.

Larsen Fund. Time and Life Bldg., Room 3436, New York, N.Y. 10020. (212) 841-2665.

Broad purposes; grants largely for higher and secondary education and conservation; support also for a museum, hospitals, and libraries, primarily in the New York area and Massachusetts. No grants to individuals.

Lesher (Margaret and Irvin) Foundation. c/o First Seneca Bank and Trust Co., Oil City, Pa. 16301. (814) 676-6511.

Primarily local giving, with emphasis on scholarships for Clarion County Pennsylvania, students; support also for a hospital and a public library. No grants for endowment funds.

Levy (June Rockwell) Foundation, Inc. 100 Federal St., Rm. 2900, Boston, Mass. 02110.

General purposes; grants largely for medical research, higher and secondary education, hospitals, and cultural programs; support also for music, a museum, youth agencies, and the handicapped, primarily in Massachusetts and Rhode Island.

Lilly Endowment, Inc. 2801 N. Meridian St., Box 88068, Indianapolis, Ind. 46208. (317) 924-5471.

Giving emphasizes projects that depend on private support, with a limited number of grants to government institutions and tax-supported programs. Special interest in innovative programs that seek to produce positive changes in human society, promote human development, strengthen independent institutions, encourage responsive government at local, state, and national levels, and improve the quality of life in Indianapolis and Indiana. Grants for cultural programs limited to Indianapolis and Indiana.

Lincoln National Life Foundation, Inc., The. 1300 S. Clinton St., Fort Wayne, Ind. 46801. (219) 424-5421.

General purposes; maintains the Lincoln Library and Museum; grants primarily for health research and to higher educational institutions. No grants to individuals or for endowment funds.

Longwood Foundation, Inc. 2024 DuPont Bldg., Wilmington, Del. 19898. (302) 654-2477.

Primary obligation is the support, operation, and development of Longwood Gardens, which are open to the public; some assistance to Eleutherian Mills Historical Library in Wilmington; limited grants generally to nearby educational institutions for scientific and engineering training and to local hospitals for construction purposes. No grants to individuals or for special projects.

Loutit Foundation, The. Grand Haven, Mich. 49417. (616) 842-7110.

Broad purposes; primarily concerned with programs and projects related to the welfare of the citizens in the Grand Haven area of western Michigan.

Lumpkin Foundation, The. c/o R. A. Lumpkin, 121 S. 17 St., Mattoon, Ill. 61938. (217) 235-3361.

Broad purposes; grants primarily for higher education, hospitals, and health agencies; support also for public libraries. No grants to individuals.

Markey (The John C.) Charitable Fund. Box 191, Bryan, Ohio 43506.

Grants for higher and secondary education, Protestant church support, hospitals, and libraries, primarily in Ohio.

Marshall (Harriet McDaniel) Trust in Memory of Sanders McDaniel. c/o Trust Company Bank, Box 4418, Atlanta, Ga. 30302.

Primarily local giving, with emphasis on a building fund for a higher educational institution, aid to the handicapped, and community funds. No grants to individuals.

Martin Foundation, Inc., The. 500 Simpson St., Elkhart, Ind. 46514.

Broad purposes; primarily local giving, with emphasis on construction of a public library, church support, community funds, youth agencies, and education. No grants to individuals.

*Mellon (The Andrew W.) Foundation. 140 E. 62 St., New York, N.Y. 10021. (212) 838-8400. *Contact*: J. Kellum Smith, Jr., Vice-Pres.

The Mellon Foundation supports a broad range of activities. Grants are awarded on a selective basis in higher education, cultural affairs, performing arts, and in certain environmental and public affairs areas. No grants or loans are given to individuals or to strictly local organizations. Most of the libraries that have received funds have been academic libraries in prominent privately supported institutions. The best way for other libraries to obtain support from the foundation is to approach it as a consortium of institutions. The foundation in 1978 and 1979 was particularly receptive to proposals to improve training of library staffs.

Milbank (The Dunlevy) Foundation, Inc. c/o Donald R. Osborn, 125 Broad St., New York, N.Y. 10004. (212) 558-3724.

Broad purposes; giving limited primarily to New York City with emphasis on support for a teaching hospital, zoological society, and public library. No grants to individuals.

Morgan City Fund, The. Box 949, Morgan City, La. 70380.

Charitable purposes; local giving only, with emphasis on parks, landscaping, and recreational facilities; support also for a public library, secondary schools, a hospital, and youth agencies.

Morrison Charitable Trust. Box 3099, Winston-Salem, N.C. 27102.

Primarily local giving, with emphasis on hospitals and libraries.

Mudd (The Seeley G.) Fund. 523 W. Sixth Street, Suite 1206, Los Angeles, Calif. 90014. (213) 626-4411. *Contact*: Luther C. Anderson, Chairperson.

Set up to provide building funds at leading privately endowed universities and colleges for libraries and scientific, medical, engineering, religious, and general classroom buildings, except for the humanities, music, and the arts. No grants to individuals, for endowment funds, or operating budgets.

Mulford (The Clarence E.) Trust. Eight Portland St., Fryeburg, Maine 04037. (207) 935-2061.

Primarily local giving in Fryeburg and neighboring towns, with emphasis on schools; grants also for church support, community services and welfare programs, libraries, and youth agencies. No grants to individuals.

Munson (W.B.) Foundation. c/o The Citizens National Bank of Denison, Denison, Tex. 75020.

Primarily local giving to Denison agencies, including youth agencies, health agency, hospital and public library; also provides scholarships for local high school graduates.

National Home Library Foundation. c/o Leonard H. Marks, 1333 New Hampshire Ave., N.W., Suite 600, Washington, D.C. 20036. (202) 293-3860.

Advocates assisting in the distribution of books, pamphlets, and documents to community groups that would not otherwise have access to libraries and other sources of printed material, either generally or on specific subjects. No grants to individuals, for building or endowment funds, or for operating budgets.

*New York Times Company Foundation, Inc., The. 229 W. 43 St., New York, N.Y. 10036 (212) 556-1091. *Contact:* Fred M. Hechinger, Pres.

The New York Times Company Foundation pursues broad purposes, with some emphasis on higher and secondary education, social welfare, cultural programs, journalism, and international affairs. Urban affairs are also an interest, especially as they involve New York City.

Norman (Andrew) Foundation. 10960 Wilshire Blvd., Suite 820, Los Angeles, Calif. 90024. (213) 879-1430.

Broad purposes; primarily local giving, with emphasis on minority group development, hospitals, higher education, humanities, conservation, arts, and community funds.

*Northwest Area Foundation (formerly Louis W. and Maud Hill Family Foundation). West 975 First National Bank Bldg., Saint Paul, Minn. 55101. (612) 224-9635. *Contact:* John D. Taylor, Exec. Dir.

The purpose of the Northwest Area Foundation is to aid in the development of new knowledge, to develop and improve liaison between research and practice, to encourage utilization of existing knowledge, to assist pioneering organizations in the fields of the arts and humanities, environmental and physical sciences, medical sciences and health, human services, and education. Grants are generally for experimental and demonstration projects that may have a significant impact, but for which there is not now general support. Giving is limited to Idaho, Iowa, Minnesota, Montana, North Dakota, Oregon, South Dakota, and Washington.

O'Connor (A. Lindsay and Olive B.) Foundation. Box D, Hobart, N.Y. 13788. (607) 538-9248.

Broad purposes; giving primarily in Delaware County and surrounding rural counties in upstate New York, with emphasis on "quality of life," including hospitals, libraries, community centers, higher education, mainly nursing and other vocational education, youth agencies, religious organizations, and historical restorations; support for town and village improvement and environmental improvement. No grants to individuals or for operating budgets. Ten-year report published in 1976.

Ohrstrom Foundation, Inc., The. Box 325, Middleburg, Va. 22117.

Broad purposes; general giving, largely in Virginia and New York, with emphasis on elementary and secondary education, higher education, community services, hospitals, Protestant church support, museums, libraries, and conservation.

Omaha World-Herald Foundation, The (formerly The World-Herald Foundation). c/o Omaha World-Herald Co., 14 and Dodge Sts., Omaha, Nebr. 68102. (402) 444-1000.

Broad purposes; grants limited primarily to Omaha area institutions involved with education, civic, health, welfare, and cultural programs. No grants to individuals.

Patterson (W. I.) Charitable Fund. 307 Oliver Bldg., Pittsburgh, Pa. 15222. (412) 281-5580.

Primarily local giving, with emphasis on higher education, a library, hospitals, and health and welfare funds. No grants to individuals.

Penn (The William) Foundation. 920 Suburban Sta. Bldg., 1617 John F. Kennedy Blvd., Philadelphia, Penn. 19103. (215) 568-2870.

Broad purposes; general giving, largely limited to the Philadelphia area; grants principally for educational, cultural, health, conservation, and social welfare projects. No grants to individuals or for endowment funds.

Pforzheimer (The Carl and Lily) Foundation, Inc. 70 Pine St. Rm. 3030, New York, N.Y. 10005. (212) 422-5484. *Contact*: Carl H. Pforzheimer, Jr., Pres.

General purposes; collaborates with established libraries and educational institutions in connection with the Carl H. Pforzheimer Library, acquired upon the death of one of its founders, in the general field of American and English literature; also supports charitable and educational institutions, with emphasis on higher education, medical associations, libraries, hospitals, and community agencies. No grants to individuals, for building funds, or for operating budgets.

Piper (Minnie Stevens) Foundation. 201 N. Saint Mary's St., Suite 100, San Antonio, Tex. 78205. (512) 227-8119.

Supports charitable and educational undertakings in Texas, especially to contribute toward the education of worthy students and to support community funds and other organizations or activities dedicated to the furtherance of the general welfare. An operating foundation administering a student loan fund, annual Piper Professor awards to recognize teaching excellence at the college level, Piper Scholar awards of four-year college scholarships to outstanding high school graduates in Texas, a student aid library and information center, and a scholarship clearinghouse. No grants for building or endowment funds. Report published occasionally.

Pitts (William I. H. and Lula E.) Foundation. Box 4655, Atlanta, Ga. 30302.

Broad purposes; grants primarily to Protestant churches and church-related institutions in Georgia, with emphasis on higher and secondary education, a theological school library, care of the aged, and hospitals. No grants to individuals or for endowment funds.

Price Waterhouse Foundation. 1251 Ave. of the Americas, New York, N.Y. 10020. (212) 489-8900.

The advancement of higher education in the field of accountancy; grants to colleges and universities for aid to teachers, scholarships, fellowships, and student loans, support for research programs, libraries, and other facilities.

Reynolds (Z. Smith) Foundation, Inc. 1225 Wachovia Bldg., Winston-Salem, N.C. 27101. (919) 725-7541.

General charitable purposes, limited to North Carolina; grants primarily for schools, colleges, hospitals, public health, libraries, and recreation. No grants to individuals.

Rhode Island Foundation, The. 15 Westminster St., Providence, R.I. 02903. (401) 274-4564.

Promotes educational and charitable activities that will tend to improve the living conditions and well-being of the inhabitants of Rhode Island; grants for capital and operating purposes principally to youth agencies, hospitals and health services, urban programs, educational institutions in Rhode Island for scholarships, organizations dedicated to preserving state historical landmarks, public libraries, and community funds. No grants to individuals or to sectarian institutions except as specified by the donor. No grants for endowment funds or operating budgets.

*Rockefeller Foundation, The. 1133 Ave. of the Americas, New York, N.Y. 10036. (212) 869-8500. *Contact:* Laurence D. Stifel, Sec.
Concentrates on concerns perceived to be of fundamental importance to humankind, such as hunger, population, health, international relations, education, equal opportunity, and the arts and humanities. The foundation operates primarily through grants to universities, research institutes, and other qualified agencies. No grants are awarded for establishment, building, or operation of local institutions or for personal aid to individuals.

Rubinstein (Helena) Foundation, Inc. 261 Madison Ave., New York, N.Y. 10016. (212) 986-0806. *Contact:* Mrs. Diane Corbin, Exec. Dir.
Grants worldwide in areas of education, community services, the arts, and health and medicine. Focus remains on the rights and welfare of women and children, quality health care and research essential to it, new directions in education and the arts, and the developing role of women in society. No grants to individuals or for building or endowment funds. Report published annually. Grant application guidelines available; initial approach by letter; submit one copy of proposal; board meets semiannually in November and April or May.

Sears (Clara Endicott) Trust. c/o New England Merchants National Bank, 28 State St., Boston, Mass. 02106. (617)742-4000.
Giving largely restricted to "Fruitlands and the Wayside Museums, Inc."; some support for charities in Worcester and Suffolk counties. No grants to individuals.

Second Champlin Foundation Trust, The. Bank of Delaware, 300 Delaware Ave., Wilmington, Del. 19899. (302) 429-1415.
Charitable purposes; grants largely for youth agencies, hospitals, and higher and secondary education; some support also for aid to the handicapped, community funds, and homes for the aged, primarily in Rhode Island.

Sewell (Warren P. and Ava F.) Foundation. Bremen, Ga. 30110.
Charitable and educational purposes; grants primarily to churches, hospitals, community funds, and youth agencies in Georgia.

Sherman Foundation. Box 1715, 2077 W. Coast Hwy., Newport Beach, Calif. 92663.

An operating foundation maintaining a research institute on the history of the Pacific southwest, including a library and gardens; maintains a local experimental nursery.

Slemp Foundation, The. c/o W. C. Edmonds, Big Stone Gap, Va. 24219. (513) 852-4585. (Mailing add.: c/o The First National Bank of Cincinnati, Box 1118, Cincinnati, Ohio 45201.

Charitable and educational purposes; maintenance of three named institutions; improvement of health of residents of Lee and Wise counties, Virginia, or their descendants wherever located; primarily local giving with emphasis on scholarships, a museum, higher and secondary education, libraries, and hospitals.

Snow (The John Ben) Foundation, Inc. Box 376, Pulaski, N.Y. 13142.

Support primarily for private educational institutions, youth agencies, libraries, hospitals, and community betterment projects in central New York State. Applications for grants not invited. No grants to individuals or for operating budgets.

Spencer Foundation, The. 875 N. Michigan Ave., Chicago, Ill. 60611. (312) 337-7000.

Primarily educational purposes, with emphasis on increasing knowledge about educational processes through research and applying research findings to improve educational processes. Normally no grants to individuals; no grants for building or endowment funds, or operating budgets. Focus on Illinois.

Sprague (The Seth) Educational and Charitable Foundation. c/o United States Trust Co. of New York, 45 Wall St., New York, N.Y. 10005. (212) 425-4500.

Broad purposes; general giving, largely in New York and Massachusetts, with emphasis on higher and secondary education, aid to the handicapped, medical research, hospitals and health agencies, youth and child welfare agencies, museums, church support and theological seminaries, libraries, population control, social agencies, and correctional institutions. No grants to individuals or for building or endowment funds.

Stevens (The Abbot and Dorothy H.) Foundation. Two Johnson St., North Andover, Mass. 01845.

Primarily local giving; emphasis on a library, hospitals, secondary education, music, art, and religious organizations. Grants restricted to Massachusetts with preference to the greater Lawrence area. No grants to individuals.

Surdna Foundation, Inc. 200 Park Ave., Suite 1619, New York, N.Y. 10017. (212) 697-0630.

Broad purposes; support primarily for general education, particularly higher education, medical education, health care delivery, medical research, social concerns, and cultural affairs. Focus primarily on the northeastern area of the United States. No grants to individuals or for operating budgets. Report published biennially.

Symmes (F. W.) Foundation. c/o South Carolina National Bank, Box 969, Greenville, S.C. 29602. (803) 242-6810.

Broad purposes; primarily local giving, with emphasis on church support, child welfare, hospitals, youth agencies, music, and recreation.

Temple (T. L. L.) Foundation. Box 779, Diboll, Tex. 75941.

Primarily local giving with emphasis on hospitals, child welfare, education, community funds, and libraries.

Thille (The Albert) Foundation. Box 728, Santa Paula, Calif. 93060. (805) 525-3712.

Broad purposes; primarily local giving, with emphasis on higher education, hospitals and medical aid, church support, youth agencies, and a museum. No grants to individuals except for scholarships, for endowment funds, or for operating budgets.

*Tinker Foundation Inc., The. 645 Madison Ave., New York, N.Y. 10022. (212) 421-6858. *Contact*: Miriam Williford, Program Dir.

Promotes broad purposes that contribute to better understanding among peoples of Ibero-America. Grants are given to projects in the various fields of the social sciences, such as communications, demography, regional development, management, political science, history, natural resource development, and problems of technology transfer.

Support is provided for conferences, meetings, seminars, and public affairs programs. The foundation awards postdoctoral fellowships in an annual competition. No other grants are made to individuals, for building or endowment funds, or operating budgets. Library grants have normally been given when they appeal to the subject interests of the foundation.

Trexler Foundation. 1227 Hamilton St., Box 303, Allentown, Pa. 18105. (215) 434-9645.

The will provides that one-fourth of the income shall be added to the corpus, one-fourth paid to the City of Allentown for park purposes, and the remainder distributed to such charitable organizations and objects as shall be "of the most benefit to humanity," but limited to Allentown and Lehigh County, particularly for hospitals, churches, institutions for the care of the crippled and orphans, youth agencies, and support of ministerial students at two named Pennsylvania institutions.

Van Ameringen Foundation, Inc. 509 Madison Ave., New York, N.Y. 10022. (212) 758-6221.

Grants chiefly to promote mental health and social welfare through preventive measures, treatment, and rehabilitation; some general local giving. Grants made largely in the urban Northeast although occasional awards reach other sections of the country.

*Weatherhead Foundation, The. 420 Lexington Ave., Rm. 1660, New York, N.Y. 10017. (212) 687-2130.

The foundation provides grants for endowment or programs, principally to universities or research organizations. Grants made in 1978 reflect a change in the foundation's funding interest from culture and education in the southwest and Ohio to a more general interest in higher education, museums, and cultural projects.

Western New York Foundation, The. Marine Trust Bldg., Suite 1402, Buffalo, N. Y. 14203. (716) 847-6440.

Broad purposes; grants to nondenominational, nonprofit institutions within the counties of Erie, Niagara, Genesee, Wyoming, Allegany, Cattaraugus, and Chautauqua, with emphasis on capital needs of new projects or expanding services. Support primarily for the performing arts, youth agencies, and social agencies. No grants to individuals, for endowment funds, or to religious organizations. Report published annually.

Whittenberger (Claude R. and Ethel B.) Foundation. Box 1073, Caldwell, Idaho. (208) 459-0091.

Giving limited to institutions in Idaho, with emphasis on education, religion, and health, special emphasis on youth. Support for hospitals, cultural programs, and local public library. No grants to individuals or for endowment funds.

Williams (John C.) Charitable Trust. c/o Pittsburgh National Bank, Box 340747P, Pittsburgh, Pa. 15230. (412) 355-3796.

For the benefit of the communities of Steubenville, Ohio, and Weirton, West Virginia, with emphasis on higher education, hospitals, a community center, a public library, and youth agencies. No grants to individuals.

*Wilson (The H. W.) Foundation, Inc. 950 University Ave., Bronx, N.Y. 10452. (212) 588-8400. *Contact*: Leo M. Weins, Pres., or James Humphry, III, Vice-Pres.

Broad purposes, including aid to former company employees; grants largely to library associations and accredited library schools in the United States and Canada for scholarships. No grants to individuals, for building and endowment funds, or for operating budgets. Initial approach by letter; board meets quarterly in January, March, July, and October.

Appendix 3
State Foundation Directories

Alabama. *A Guide to Foundations of the Southeast*, vol. 4, 1976. Davis-Taylor Associates, Rte. 3, Box 289, Mt. Morgan Rd., Williamsburg, Ky. 40769. $25.* (126 foundations)†

Arkansas. *(104 foundations).* See Alabama

California. *Guide to California Foundations*, 1976. The San Mateo Foundation, 1204 Burlingame Ave., Rm. 10, Burlingame, Calif. 94010. $4. prepaid. (335 foundations)

Connecticut. *A Directory of Foundations in the State of Connecticut*, 3rd ed., 1976. Eastern Connecticut State College Foundation, Inc., Box 431, Willimantic, Conn. 06226. $7. prepaid. (590 foundations)

District of Columbia. *The Guide to Washington, D.C., Foundations*, 2nd ed., 1975. Guide Publishers, Box 5849, Washington, D.C. 20014. $8. (282 foundations)

Florida. *A Guide to the Foundations of the Southeast*, vol. 3, 1975. Davis-Taylor Associates, Inc., Rte. 3, Box 289, Mt. Morgan Rd., Williamsburg, Ky. 40769. $25. (487 foundations)

*Prices subject to change.

†Indicates number of foundations listed in the particular directory.

114

Georgia. (340 foundations). See Florida.

Illinois. *Illinois Foundation Profiles,* 1976. Davis-Taylor Associates, Inc., Rte. 3, Box 289, Mt. Morgan Rd., Williamsburg, Ky. 40769. $29.95. (319 foundations)

Indiana. *A Guide to Indiana Foundations,* 1975. Davis-Taylor Associates, Inc. Rte. 3, Box 289, Mt. Morgan Rd., Williamsburg, Ky. 40769. $29.95. (334 foundations)

Kansas. *Directory of Kansas Foundations,* 1975. Association of Community Arts Councils of Kansas, 117 W. Tenth St., Suite 100, Topeka, Kans. 66612. $1.25. (205 foundations)

Kentucky. *A Guide to Foundations of the Southeast,* vol. 1, 1975. Davis-Taylor Associates, Inc., Rte. 3, Box 289, Mt. Morgan Rd., Williamsburg, Ky. 40769. $25. (119 foundations)

Louisiana. (172 foundations). See Alabama

Maine. *Directory of Maine Foundations,* 2nd ed., 1975. Eastern Connecticut State College Foundation, Inc., Box 431, Willimantic, Conn. 06226. $5. prepaid. (62 foundations)

Maryland. *1975 Annual Index Foundation Reports,* 1976. Office of the Attorney-General, One Calvert St., 14 fl., Baltimore, Md. 21202. $3.20. (278 foundations)

Massachusetts. *A Directory of Foundations in the Commonwealth of Massachusetts,* 1974. Eastern Connecticut State College Foundation, Inc., Box 431, Willimantic, Conn. 06226. $11. prepaid. (998 foundations)

Directory of the Major Greater Boston Foundations, 1974. J. F. Gray Co., Box 748, Islington Sta., Westwood, Mass. 02090. $14.95 plus postage. (47 Boston area foundations)

Michigan. *Michigan Foundation Directory,* 1976. Michigan League for Human Services, 200 Mill St., Lansing, Mich. 48933. $5. prepaid. (267 foundations)

Directory of Foundations in the State of Michigan, 1974. Dunham Pond Press, Storrs, Conn. 06268. $10. (696 foundations)

Minnesota. *Minnesota Foundation Directory III: Guidelines and Deadlines,* 1975. Minnesota Foundation Directory III, Suite 305, Peavey Bldg., Minneapolis, Minn. 55402. $50. (55 foundations)

Mississippi. (68 foundations). See Alabama

New Hampshire. *A Directory of Foundations in the State of New Hampshire,* 2nd ed., 1975. Eastern Connecticut State College Foundation, Inc., Box 431, Willimantic, Conn. 06226. $5. prepaid (138 foundations)

Directory of Charitable Funds in New Hampshire, 3rd ed., 1976. Office of the Attorney-General, State House Annex, Concord, N. H. 03301. $2. (approx. 400 foundations)

North Carolina. *A Guide to Foundations of the Southeast,* vol. 2, 1975. Davis-Taylor Associates, Inc., Rte. 3, Box 289, Mt. Morgan Rd., Williamsburg, Ky. 40769. $25. (415 foundations)

Ohio. *Charitable Foundations Directory of Ohio,* 2nd ed., 1975. Office of the Attorney-General, 30 E. Broad St., 15 fl., Columbus, Ohio 43215. $4. prepaid. (2,500 foundations)

Oklahoma. *Directory of Oklahoma Foundations,* 1974. University of Oklahoma Press, 1005 Asp Ave., Norman, Okla. 73069. $9.95. (269 foundations)

Oregon. *Directory of Foundations and Charitable Trusts Registered in Oregon* (1972 data). Dept. of Justice, 555 State Office Bldg., 1400 S.W. Fifth Ave., Portland, Oreg. 97201. $5. prepaid. (331 foundations)

Pennsylvania. *Directory of Charitable Organizations,* 1974. Office of the Attorney-General, Capitol Annex, Harrisburg, Pa. 17120. Out of print. (approx. 1,200 foundations)

Rhode Island. *A Directory of Foundations in the State of Rhode Island,* 2nd ed., 1975. Eastern Connecticut State College Foundation, Inc., Box 431, Willimantic, Conn. 06226. $5. prepaid. (117 foundations)

South Carolina. (131 foundations). See North Carolina

Tennessee. (238 foundations). See Kentucky

Texas. *Directory of Texas Foundations,* 1976. Texas Foundations Research Center, 306 W. 29 St., Austin, Tex. 78705. $10.95 prepaid. (1,020 foundations)

The Guide to Texas Foundations, 1975. Southern Resource Center, Box 5593, Dallas, Tex. 75222. $7.50, includes postage and handling. (214 foundations)

Vermont. *A Directory of Foundations in the State of Vermont*, 1975. Eastern Connecticut State College Foundation, Inc., Box 431, Willimantic, Conn. 06226. $3. prepaid. (41 foundations)

Virginia. (319 foundations). See Kentucky

Washington. *Charitable Trust Directory*, 1975. Office of the Attorney-General, Temple of Justice, Olympia, Wash. 98504. $3. prepaid. (458 foundations)

Wisconsin. *Foundations in Wisconsin: A Directory*, 1976. Marquette University Memorial Library, 1415 W. Wisconsin Ave., Milwaukee, Wis. 53233. $10. prepaid. (700 foundations)

Appendix 4

Federal Sources of Grants

Department of Agriculture (USDA)*
14 St. and Independence Ave.
Washington, D. C. 20250

Department of Commerce*
Constitution Ave. and E. St., N.W.
Washington, D.C. 20230
Economic Development Administration
National Oceanic and Atmospheric Administration

Department of Defense (DOD)*
The Pentagon
Washington, D. C. 20301
Air Force Office of Scientific Research
Army Research Institute
Office of Navy Research

Department of Education †
Office of Libraries and Learning Technologies

400 Maryland Ave., S.W.
Washington, D.C. 20202

Department of Energy (DOE)*
Washington, D.C. 20585

Department of Health, Education, and Welfare (HEW)*
200 Independence Ave., S.W.
Washington, D.C. 20202
Food and Drug Administration
Fund for Improvement of Past Secondary Education
Health Resources Administration
Health Service Administration
National Institute of Education
National Institutes of Health
Office of Education

Department of Housing and Urban Development (HUD)*
451 Seventh St., S.W.
Washington, D.C. 20410

*Federal agency that has funded libraries.

†Principal source of information on government library support.

Note: HEW, as of June 1980, reorganized as the Department of Education and Department of Human Services.

118

Department of the Interior*
18 and C Sts., N.W.
Washington, D.C. 20240
  Bureau of Indian Affairs
  National Park Service

Department of Justice*
Washington, D.C. 20520

Department of Labor (DOL)*
Third and Constitution Ave., N.W.
Washington, D.C. 20210
  Manpower Administration

Department of State*
Washington, D.C. 20523

Department of Transportation*
415 12 St., N.W.
Washington, D.C. 20004
  University Research Program
  Urban Mass Transit Administration

National Aeronautics and Space Administration (NASA)*
400 Maryland Ave., S.W.
Washington, D.C. 20546

National Archives[†]
National Historical Publications and
  Records Commission
Washington, D.C. 20408

**National Endowment for the Arts
  (NEA)** *[†]
General Information
2401 E. St., N.W.
Washington, D.C. 20506

National Endowment for the Humanities (NEH) *[†]
Public Information Office
Washington, D.C. 20506

National Institute of Education (NIE) [†]
1200 19 St., N.W.
Washington, D.C. 20208

National Library of Medicine [†]
Extramural Programs
Bethesda, Md. 20014

National Science Foundation (NSF) *[†]
Division of Information Science and
  Technology
Washington, D.C. 20550

*Federal agency that has funded libraries.
[†]Principal source of information on government library support.

Appendix 5

Federal Regional Centers

Region I: Connecticut, Maine, Massachusetts, New Hampshire, Rhode Island, Vermont
John F. Kennedy Federal Bldg.
Government Center
Boston, Mass. 02203

Region II: New Jersey, New York, Puerto Rico, Virgin Islands
26 Federal Plaza, Rm. 1005
New York, N.Y. 10007

Region III: Delaware, Maryland, Pennsylvania, Virginia, West Virginia, Washington, D.C.
Box 13716
Philadelphia, Pa. 19101

Region IV: Alabama, Florida, Georgia, Kentucky, Mississippi, North Carolina, South Carolina, Tennessee
50 Seventh St., N.E., Rm. 404
Atlanta, Ga. 30323

Region V: Illinois, Indiana, Michigan, Minnesota, Ohio, Wisconsin
300 S. Wacker Dr., 34 fl.
Chicago, Ill. 60606

Region VI: Arkansas, Louisiana, New Mexico, Oklahoma, Texas
1114 Commerce St.
Dallas, Tex. 75202

Region VII: Iowa, Kansas, Missouri, Nebraska
601 E. 12 St.
Kansas City, Mo. 64106

Region VIII: Colorado, Montana, North Dakota, South Dakota, Utah, Wyoming
9017 Federal Office Bldg.
19 and Stout Sts.
Denver, Colo. 80202

Region IX: Arizona, California, Guam, Hawaii, Nevada, American Samoa, Trust Territory of the Pacific Islands
50 Fulton St.
San Francisco, Calif. 94102

Region X: Alaska, Idaho, Oregon, Washington
Arcade Plaza Bldg.
1321 Second Ave.
Seattle, Wash. 98101

Note: Regions listed in this appendix were established by HEW as administrative regions. They are subject to change under the current Department of Education.

Glossary

A-95 Clearinghouse. A procedure requiring local and state-level officials to look over and comment on applications being made to any of more than 200 federal funding programs. This preliminary review assures that proposed projects conform to equal opportunity and environmental protection legislation and, most importantly, that they do not duplicate other federally funded projects already in existence.

Accountability. Emphasis on keeping careful accounting of where grant money goes, how it is spent, and whether it seems to have had an effect on the problem it was intended to help resolve.

Applied Research. Research undertaken to attempt to resolve human problems, rather than simply to add to the sum of human knowledge. See also Basic Research.

Approval/Disapproval Time. The length of time it takes a funder to review proposals and make decisions on them.

Authorization. The legislation that establishes a basis for the inception of a government program.

Basic Research. Research oriented toward simply expanding knowledge. See also Applied Research.

Block Grant. Federal grants made under very broad, general subject areas; for example, Community Development. Decisions about the ultimate allocation of these funds are left to the discretion, within limits, of local or regional authorities. See also Categorical Grant.

Boilerplate. Sections of any document, especially a proposal, that have been used and reused so often that they have become standardized elements that change very little if at all with each new use. Resumes used in personnel sections of proposals are a good example.

Categorical Grant. Federal grant made under narrow, specific program guidelines that carefully spell out such matters as eligibility requirements, program time frames, and intended beneficiaries. Much less discretion about the distribution of categorical grants is left to local or state authorities than is common under Block Grants.

Challenge Grant. Also known as Matching Grant. Offered by a funder with the express stipulation that the prospective grantee organization must locate another funder who will share a percentage (usually ranging from 10 to 50 percent) of the project costs. Used by many federal and some foundation grant programs to indicate a wide local support for the intended project.

Client. Individual or group who ultimately receives the services that the grant is intended to support.

Community Foundation. See Foundation.

Contingency Funding. Support offered with a catch—one has to comply with certain requirements before qualifying for the money.

Contract. An agreement, usually in writing, summarizing the understanding between the funding source and a recipient of a grant or contract. It is usually prepared after the negotiations have been completed. The contract need not be so labeled; it is often called a letter of agreement.

Data Collection Procedures. Systems established, usually at the start of a project, to keep track of project operations so that its effectiveness and efficiency can later be analyzed.

Defunding. A bureaucratic euphemism meaning "your funding has been cut."

Demonstration Grant. A grant made to set up an innovative project that will function as a model and that, if successful, will be duplicated in other locations and other fields by different grantees.

Direct Costs. The specific, identifiable costs of operating a grant-supported project. See also Indirect Costs.

Discretionary Funds. Grants allocated according to a funder's judgment rather than according to a pre-established guideline or set of criteria.

Dissemination. The act of seeing that the results of the project are made widely available so that others may learn from it.

Documentation/Record-keeping. The paper trail that any project generates in keeping track of its staff, clients, services, and budget.

Donor Control. Something of an issue in the foundation world. One camp believes that donors should have relatively little to say about where their money goes, since they tend to indulge their biases and give very idiosyncratically (see also Vanity Funding). The opposing point of view is that donors who in the past have kept careful control over the eventual allocations of their gifts have neither a worse nor a better record for making good grants than any other group.

Effectiveness. Does it work?

Efficiency. How well does it operate?

Endowment. The sum of money that is made available to a foundation by a donor and is then invested so as to provide funds out of which grants are made, taxes paid, operating expenses met, and so forth.

Evaluation. The process of comparing what a project set out to do with what it actually accomplished.

Formula Grant. A grant that apportions funds among localities solely on the basis of such factors as population, number of people living below the poverty level, tax "effort," urbanization, and so forth.

Foundation. A foundation is in essence: (1) an endowment, contributed by a donor, which is invested so as to realize an income from which grants are made, and (2) a board or committee that reviews proposals and decides where the money will be placed. There are two general categories of foundation: public and private. Private foundations can be further subdivided into general purpose, special purpose, family, and operating. Public foundations are synonymous with community foundations.

Funder. Any person, institution, or agency that makes grants. Usually subdivided into three major categories: government agencies, foundations, and corporations.

Funding Cycle. The pattern of announcement, proposal review, and grantee notification that characterizes any funder.

Funding Period. The length of time that the grant covers, most often one year, with a possibility of renewal; rarely more than three years.

Giving Pattern. The overall configuration of the kind of projects that the funder has supported in the past, where they are located, how much money they have received, and what kind of organizations have conceived, sponsored, and managed them.

Goal. The broad, general, all-inclusive social change that the grant is intended to foster and the project is designed to help achieve.

Grant. A one-way, voluntary transfer of money or other economic goods or services from a funder to a grantee, made in order to support the philanthropic activities outlined by the grantee in the proposal.

Grantee. The group, or, rarely, individual, that receives the grant from the funder.

Grants-in-Aid. A synonym for grant.

Grants Officer. The individual in a funding agency who is responsible for direct administration of a grant program.

Grantsmanship. The knack of knowing where the money is and how to get at it.

Grievance Procedure. Procedures established by federal granting programs for applicants who are turned down.

Guidelines. A funder's statement of its goals, priorities, eligibility criteria, and application procedures, or those of one of its programs.

Hard Match. Money, rather than facilities or services required to match. See also Soft Match.

Implemented. Actually put into practice or operation.

In Kind. Describes contributions other than money, usually services, facilities, or equipment.

Indirect Costs. A budget category that is intended to cover those general administrative costs of operating a project that are hard to assign to specific project functions. Typically, these costs include building rent and maintenance, depreciation, general local travel, and so forth. See also Direct Costs.

Joint Funding. It is not uncommon for grant projects to be supported by more than one funder, each of whom either may provide support for one self-contained component of the overall project or may contribute to a common pool of grant funds.

Letter of Intent/Inquiry. The first contact with a prospective funder often takes this form rather than a phone call. Briefly states one's intention to apply for funds and gives a very brief idea of the nature of the planned project.

Letter of Support. Written statements attached to the back of proposals, provided by organizations and individuals who endorse a project's efforts.

Matching Grant. See Challenge Grant.

Needs Assessment. Perhaps the most critical component of the proposal, the section that answers the question "Why is this project needed?"

Nonprofit Corporation. The predominant organizational form of grant recipients.

OMB Circulars. Instructions, guidelines, and directions issued to all federal grant-making programs by the Office of Management and Budget.

Objectives. The proposal's goals must be translated into specific, quantified targets or levels of achievement to provide a set of criteria by which the success or failure of the project can be judged.

Operating Foundation. A fund or endowment designated by the Internal Revenue Service as a private foundation that undertakes the operation of research, social welfare, or other programs. Few external grants are made.

Overhead. See Indirect Costs

Pass-through Agency. An intermediary that accepts funds from one source and distributes them to another. State departments and agencies play a prominent pass-through role in reallocating federal grant funds, particularly under block programs.

Peer Review. Critical reading of a proposal or contract by reputable practitioners and others conversant with the field it addresses, who are in a position to judge the competence of the applicant. See also Technical Review.

Private Foundation. See Foundation.

Proposal. The written application for grant funds.

Public Foundation. See Foundation.

RFP. Request for Proposal; the public notice that is issued by a funder who wishes to procure a service from a contractor.

Revenue Sharing. Essentially, a massive formula grant program that the Department of the Treasury has been operating since 1972. Money collected from individual income taxes is returned to local municipalities for redistribution as local authorities determine, within broad limits.

Rules and Regulations. Once authorizing legislation for a federal grant program has been passed by Congress, the actual details of its operation are set forth in the *Federal Register* under this heading.

Set-aside. Grant funds earmarked in advance for specific groups, or even specific single recipients, usually as a result of effective lobbying.

Sign-off. An authorized representative of one's sponsor (or fiscal agent) will have to put his or her signature on a variety of documents for them to be approved by the funder, especially if it is a government agency.

Site Visit. It is not uncommon for a funder to want to visit the actual project facilities, to talk with the staff, take a look around, and generally get the feel of the applicant's organization.

Soft Match. Service, facilities, equipment—in short, anything but money. See also Hard Match.

Solicited Proposal. A proposal that has specifically been requested by the granting agency to perform work conceived by the agency.

Sponsor. An agency or institution that undertakes to assist and support a grantee by offering it credibility and perhaps also services or space, but not money.

Subcontract. An arrangement by which the direct recipient of the funds has part of the work done by another individual or organization.

Tax Exempt. A status bestowed by the Internal Revenue Service and the individual states on organizations that have adequately demonstrated a charitable, educational, religious, scientific, or literary nature.

Technical Review. Critical reading of a proposal or contract by specialists whithin its content area to determine its congruence with the state of the art. See also Peer Review.

Unexpended Funds. What is left in a funder's grant-making budget as the year draws to a close.

Unrestricted Funds. Grants made without prior stipulations as to their use, to be spent as the grantee sees fit.

Unsolicited Applications. Although most government funding programs operate according to the firm deadlines, disseminated in program announcements and in the *Catalog of Federal Domestic Assistance*, some do not, and neither do most foundation and corporate grantors. Submissions to these funding programs are called unsolicited applications.

Vanity funding. Funding motivated by a desire to gratify the funder's ego and dramatize his or her existence rather than by genuine altruism. See also Donor Control.

Bibliography

Abarbanel, Karin. "Using the Grants Index to Plan a Funding Search." *Foundation News* 17: 1 (January–February 1976).

Allen, Herb, ed. *The Bread Game: The Realities of Foundation Fund Raising*. San Francisco: Glide Publications, 1974.

American Library Association. *Funding Alternatives for Libraries* Chicago: ALA, 1979.

Annual Register of Grants Support. Chicago: Marquis Who's Who (latest edition)

Baker, Keith. "The New Contractmanship." *Grantsmanship Center News* (March–April 1976).

Battle, Joseph; Melville, C. Bruce; Connell, Kenneth; Taffe, Donna; and Kramer, Ed. "How to Develop an Effective Fund-Raising Strategy." *Grantsmanship Center News* (August–October 1976).

Beasley, Kenneth L. "Information Sources for Research Administrators." *Journal of the Society of Research Administrators 8:2 (Fall 1976)*.

Belcher, Jane C., and Jacobsen, Julia M. *A Process for the Development of Ideas*. Washington, D.C: Government Relations Office, 1976.

Brodsky, Jane, ed. *Proposal Writers' Swipe File*. Washington, D.C: Taft Products, Inc., Non Profit Ability Series, 1976.

Catalog of Federal Domestic Assistance. Washington, D.C.: Government Printing Office (latest edition).

Commerce Business Daily. Washington, D.C.: Government Printing Office (latest edition).

Conrad, Daniel L. *How to Get Federal Grants*. San Francisco: Public Management Institute, 1979.

DeBakey, Lois. "The Persuasive Proposal." *Foundation News* 18: 4 (July–August 1977).

Double 500 Directory. Trenton, N.J.; Fortune (latest edition).

Drennar, Henry T. "Library Legislation Discovered." *Library Trends* 24:1 (July 25, 1975), 101–115.

Federal Aid Planner: A Guide for School District Administrators. Arlington, Va: National School Public Relations Association, 1976.

Federal Funding Guide for Elementary and Secondary Education. Washington, D.C: Education Funding Research Council, 1974–1975.

Financial Assistance by Geographic Area. Washington, D.C.: HEW (latest edition).

Flanagan, Joan. *The Grass Roots Fundraising Book: How to Raise Money in Your Community*. Chicago: The Swallow Press, 1977.

Foundation Annual Reports: What They Are and How to Use Them. New York: Foundation Center (latest edition).

Foundation Center Source Book Profiles. New York: Foundation Center. (latest edition).

Foundation Directory. New York: The Foundation Center (latest edition).

Foundation Grants Index. New York: The Foundation Center (latest edition).

Foundation News. Washington, D.C.: Council on Foundations (latest edition).

Funding Resources for Voluntary Programs. Richmond, Va: State Office on Volunteerism, Fourth Street Office Building, (September, 1976).

Gansneder, Bruce M. "Program Evaluation," In *Planning and Assessment in Community Education*, edited by Harold J. Burbach, and Larry E. Decker, Midland, Mich: Pendell Publishing., 1977.

Gold, Norman. "Preparing an Evaluation Proposal," In *Proposal Development Handbook*. Baltimore, Md: Center for the Study of Volunteerism, University of Maryland, 1971.

Government Contracts and Grants for Research: A Guide for Colleges and Universities. Washington, D.C: Committee on Governmental Relations, National Association of College and University Business Officers, 1975.

Grants Administration Manual. Washington, D.C: HEW Department Staff Manual, 1976.

Grantsmanship Center News. Los Angeles: Grantsmanship Center (latest edition).

The Grantsmanship Workplan. Canoga, Calif.: The Eckman Center, 1975.

Hall, Mary. *Developing Skills in Proposal Writing*, 2nd ed. Portland, Oreg.: Continuing Education Publications, 1977.

Hillman, Howard, and Abarbanel, Karin. *The Art of Winning Foundation Grants.* New York: Vanguard Press, 1975.

Improving Federal Grants Management. Washington, D.C: Advisory Commission on Intergovernmental Relations (February 1977).

Jacquette, F. Lee, and Jacquette, Barbara I. *What Makes a Good Proposal?* New York: The Foundation Center (n.d.).

Jenkins, Patricia. "Guide to the New Grants Administration Standards for Non-Profits." *Grantsmanship Center News.* (November–December 1976).

Lewis, Marianna O., ed. *The Foundation Directory.* New York: The Foundation Center, 1975.

Million Dollar Directory. New York: Dun and Bradstreet (latest edition).

Morgolin, Judith B. *About Foundations.* New York: The Foundation Center, 1975.

National Data Book. New York: The Foundation Center (latest edition).

Pallante, James J.; McLaughlin, Gerald W.; and Smart, John C. "A Role Analysis of Higher Education Grant Administrators," *Journal of the Society of Research Administrators* 6:2 (Fall, 1974).

Proposal Development Handbook. Baltimore, Md: Center for the Study of Volunteerism, University of Maryland, 1971.

Putting It Together: A Guide to Proposal Development. Chicago: The Board of Education of the City of Chicago, 1975.

Russell, John M. *Giving and Taking Across the Foundation Desk.* New York: Columbia University Teachers College Press, 1977.

Saasta, Timothy. "How Foundations Review Proposals and Make Grants—Part I." *Grantsmanship Center News* (November–December 1976).

Urgo, Louis. *A Manual for Obtaining Government Grants.* Boston: Robert J. Corcoran, 1970.

Utech, Ingrid. *Stalking the Large Green Giant: A Fund Raising Manual for Youth Serving Agencies.* Washington, D.C: National Youth Alternatives Project, 1976

Warm, Harriet. "How Grantseekers Lower the Odds." *Foundation News* (July–August 1979), 20–21, 37–43.

Williams, Walker A., and Co. *Resource Development in the Private Sector: A Technical Assistance Manual.* Washington, D.C: Produced under contract administered by American Bicentennial Administration, 1976.

White, Virginia. *Grants: How to Find Out about Them and What to Do Next.* New York: Plenum Press, 1975.

Wilhelm, F. S. *A Manual of Policies and Procedures for Sponsored Research.* Eugene, Oreg.: Office of Scientific and Scholarly Research, University of Oregon (n.d.).

Willner, William, and Hendricks, Perry B., Jr. *Grants Administration.* Washington, D.C: National Graduate University, 1972.

Willner, William, and Nichols, John P. *Handbook of Grants and Contracts for Non Profit Organizations.* Woodward, Okla.: Bethesda Research Institute, 1976.

Zallen, Harold, and Robl, Richard. *Planning for Research and Sponsored Programs: A Guide and Resource Book.* Stillwater, Okla.: Oklahoma State University, 1973.

Zallen, Harold, and Zallen, Eugenia M. *Ideas Plus Dollars.* Norman, Okla.: Academic World, 1976.

Index

131